Neuro I

Dan

Stories from BLANKETS MOUNTAIN

Year Two – Living Life to the Fullest

Eric and Amanda Fish

Dedicated to:

Danielle Schaefer-Zoellner (Gramma)

Prologue

Hai my furiends. I am ready to start telling you more stories. I'm really excited about it, but Mum said that I have to remember that I might have new friends who are reading my stories who might not have had a chance to learn about me yet. That means I should take a moment to tell everyone a little about me. I love to tell my stories and I really want to jump into telling them so I am going to let mum explain my condition. Some of those words are a bit much for me to try to pronounce anyways. Below is a post mum put up on my Facebook page in February of 2016. She posted it because I had made hundreds and hundreds of new friends. A cold front was coming in and it made my neurological issues flare up. I let everyone know that I wasn't feeling good. Once I did that I got a lot messages from my new friends who didn't understand. Here is the post that mum made to explain it to all of my new friends.

If this is the first time I'm getting to meet you… Well Hi! It's nice to meet you and welcome to the family. I hope what mum wrote helps you understand my special needs.

Hi friends. Dan's mum here.

After last night's post there were a ton of questions about Dan's health and why he doesn't feel good. I think it is easier to write a post about him rather than try to answer all the questions, which I don't mind answering at all.

Dan has a diagnosis of progressive motor neuron disease that affects his muscles from the ribs up. This means his brain can't tell his muscles what to do. It is congenital and there is no cure. There is also no medicinal therapy to prolong his life. He has seen 4 vets as well as top notch vets at Auburn University.

His prognosis is poor to grave and they gave him a year and a half to 2 years to live, which is just a number. He has already lasted longer than everyone told us he would. He is not in pain. He loves life and is the most loving soul we have ever come across. It seems he has better days when the weather is warm. Dan is a fighter and doesn't let his disease get him down. He always surprises us with his new ways to negotiate his disAbilities.

He is a slow eater so we spend about an hour 2x a day feeding him. My husband is wonderful at finding ways to stimulate him to play in different ways. It seems stress causes his condition to progress rapidly in stages so we avoid having company that could be loud. My mother has been an integral part of his life. When we are not home she comes over to feed him. We will continue to fight for him until he no longer wants to fight. Much love to all of you and thank you for loving him.

Chapter One – Nursing the Parents

Neuro Dan - Feather Dan

January 11, 2016 ·
Hai my furiends. Today I went on an adventure across the couch and discovered that I can get between the cushions and play. It also makes for a new place for me to play hide and seek with mum! He-he Iz still keeping everyone on their toes. Loves you all and sleep with the angels my friends.

Hai my furiends! I had a good day today. I've been doing what I said I would at the end of my last book. I've been gathering my thoughts and remembering some of my favorite stories. Year two was one busy year. I had a lot of ups and a couple of downs but mostly I had a lot of fun. I sure do have a lot of great memories to choose from! Today I got a notion and decided it was time to share some stories again.

Do you remember the last story I was telling you? Christmas had come and gone. New Year's Eve had arrived and I got to enjoy another first. That first was the first time I got to spend the night snuggled in bed between mum and dad. That was when I discovered that one of those traditions I was learning about was that on New Year's Eve there sure were a lot of fireworks. Our neighbors set off a lot of them that night.

While I was taking comfort in being safe in the bed with mum and dad I decided that I was going to use my stories to spread love all over the world. I was filled with excitement and anticipation about the New Year. I was curious to see how many more friends I would get to make. I wanted to see how many times I could help others like others had helped me. I was excited about life in general and couldn't wait to see how many more adventures I'd have and how many new treats I would get to try.

That night poor Grace stayed under the bed until dad got up the next morning. She was not a fan of the fireworks any more than I was, but she was much better when she woke up. I couldn't even tell if she remembered that they had been going off. Once dad got up he gave me some chin scritches, then picked me up and took me out to my bathroom spot on the couch. It was a good thing he did too because I had been doing the best that I could not to have an accident or leave a surprise on their bed.

Grace scrambled out from under the bed and followed him out with me. Leroy and Amelia were on the table next to their food bowl waiting for their breakfast. Dad got a scoop of food and filled their bowl up. Then he got Graces leash and they disappeared out the front door for her morning walk. Mum got up and came out before dad got back. She looked around for me, saw me doing my business, and told me good morning. She told me that I'd been a good boy and maybe dad wouldn't worry about messes in the bed next time. She then got her cup of coffee and sat down at her desk.

When dad came back in mum told him she felt like she was getting sick. He went to get himself a cup of coffee and told her the same thing. The flu had been going around and they were both hoping it would just be a normal cold. Uh oh, I was about to have to take care of two sick parents and at the same time! This was going to be a challenge but I planned on recruiting Leroy, Amelia and Grace to help out. I was always up for any challenge.

By the end of the day, they were both crashed on the couch looking pretty miserable. I still managed to get some extra treats and I didn't even have to ask for them. I made sure to keep purring as much as I could because that always made mum feel better. Mum told me that it made dad feel better too, but he was grumpier than she was when he got sick. She said he was suffering from what she called a "man cold". She told me it was just like any other cold but he did a little more groaning about it than she did.

Over the next couple of days, I tried everything I could think of to help them feel better. I shared my feathers, I didn't beg for treats (but got lots anyway), and I gave extra wet face mushes. I even made sure I ate my food fast so they wouldn't have to sit there for a long time. My Facebook friends even tried to help me out. One of my friends even made a picture of me looking like a pirate that made mum and dad laugh. I saw that and spent the rest of the night trying to make them laugh with butt wiggles which mum said made it look like I was doing an Elvis impersonation. I wasn't sure who Elvis was, but I figured he must have been pretty cute.

By the end of the week they were feeling much better. Mum told me I had been an excellent nurse. She told me that all of those extra snuggles and wet face mushes helped very much. Dad must have appreciated it too because he got out a brand new bag of Temptations that were called blissful catnip flavor. Leroy and Amelia enjoyed them too. He gave us lots of them, and when he was done Amelia lay down and rolled around on the floor, showing off her belly. Leroy raced off with the zoomies and spent a half hour running back and forth across the house.

Once they were feeling better, they must have had lots of work to get caught up on because the next day they both left extra early. I didn't worry about missing my breakfast though because I knew that meant I would get a visit from Gramma. And sure enough, I was right. She came over at lunch time and we had a nice lunch date. She also made sure we got extra treats. She grabbed the catnip treats dad had opened the night before. Before she went home she got a good laugh out of Leroy and his zoomies. Leroy got lucky that Grace didn't go cop dog and get her with the pit maneuver, but Gramma was smart. She had given Grace a new chew bone as soon as she saw him get started. Grace was more interested in tossing it in the air, pouncing on it and then chomping it than she was in going after Leroy.

That weekend dad said that football was going to be even more fun. He said it was time for the playoffs. He explained what that meant to me and I had to admit it did sound like it was going to be exciting. Mum told me he would have all kinds of yummy food to eat and maybe I could sneak a bite. She warned me to stay away from those hot wings though. Mum told me that there would be an even bigger feast once the playoffs were done and the Super Bowl got there. She said she would even open up a new bag of treats from Europe for that night so I could party with them. I noticed that even mum got more interested in the games during the playoffs. That made it extra fun because I got bonus snuggles from both of them.

It was around this time that I started writing the phrase "Sleep with the Angels." It would become my way of saying goodnight at the end of my posts. Some of my friends said it was a sweet way for me to sign off for the night. Mum and I didn't know how that phrase had been used in the past. Neither of us had ever heard of it being used as a way of inferring someone should die. Mum never watched many mobster movies and she meant for it to be a comforting way of telling people that I hoped they would be watched over by the angels while they slept.

Some of my friends got confused and one night there was an argument on my Facebook page about it. Mum didn't care for the arguing because my page is supposed to just be about giving love to each other. When I heard her telling dad about it I got sad for a minute. I told mum to tell everyone not to argue. I told her to explain what it was supposed to mean so everyone would understand. Of course my friends are all loving people and things settled down again right away.

The next day my neurological issues weren't bothering me as much and I was feeling really good. I got a notion and went on an adventure across the couch. I was having fun walking across the very top edge. I'd start from Blankets Mountain and walk all the way down the top of the sectional where the couch faces the kitchen. When I'd get to where it turns along the wall I'd walk all the way down to the end by the lamp. That's where I usually play with dad at night and pounce on my feathers. There were always some feathers on top of the cushions there. I'd give a feather a couple of chomps and turn around and go back to Blankets Mountain.

I did it a couple of times. Mum doesn't like to see me doing that because I walk on the back edge of the couch and she always worries I'll fall off. Mum wasn't home so I was having a good time with it. I had just about made it back to Blankets Mountain when my back foot slipped and pushed on one of the couch cushions. The cushion fell over and I slipped. I slid, butt-first, down between the back of the couch and the cushion.

That was exciting for a second and I thought it was really fun. I didn't know I could get behind the cushions. I looked around and decided it was kind of like a pillow fort. I could pop up and look over the back of the couch or I could crouch down and hide. This would make another good place for me to play hide and seek with mum. New discoveries like that always made me extra happy.

I gave dad a surprise and a laugh when he came home from work. He set down his work stuff and looked around to see where I was before he took Grace out. When he didn't see me he headed towards the living room to see if I had gone on a floor adventure. When he got almost to Blankets Mountain I popped my head up to say hi. Dad laughed and of course he went into paparazzi mode. He was quick and got a picture before I could duck back down. He rubbed my head, picked me up and put me back on top of Blankets Mountain.

The next morning I got more notions and super excited. I had been jumping at some cushions that I don't normally jump on. They were a little more bouncy than the ones I normally jump on so I was having fun jumping up, climbing down, then jumping up again. Mum was watching closely because I was doing something different and I was obviously having a lot of fun. I got an extra burst of energy and decided I was going to try to jump even higher than before. I dove up to the very top of the cushion. The jump was so good I launched myself right over the top and off the back of the couch towards the kitchen. I don't have the same coordination as most cats and I wound up landing on my side.

Poor mum got really scared, made a terrible screeching noise, and came running over to me. I was trying to get myself up but she was pretty quick and she got me first. She scooped me up and started checking me out to make sure I was okay. She checked my legs, looked at my eyes and even gently rubbed on my belly and sides. I tried to tell her I was fine, but she was very insistent about being thorough with her inspection. Once she was satisfied I was okay she set me on Blankets Mountain and gave me luvins for a while.

Grace must have been worried too because when mum was done she hopped up on the couch right in front of her. She gave me a quick sniff on my nose then looked over at mum. She jumped down before mum had a chance to fuss at her. I could tell by the look on mums face that she thought Grace was being sweet and she wouldn't have fussed at her anyway.

That same day, dad was having a rough time at work. He started getting an earache that morning and it wound up getting worse and worse as the day went on. He was supposed to feed me dinner when he got home that day so I knew something wrong when he didn't come home on time. He wound up having to go to the human emergency vet. It turned out he got an ear infection and his eardrum ruptured.

By the time he got home, gramma had already come over to feed me and mum was even home. I guess it takes a long time in the human vets. Dad looked miserable and exhausted when he walked through the door. The doctor had him on the loopy drugs to help with the pain. He was completely deaf in his left ear and was having a terrible time hearing. Mum wound up having to yell at him to get his attention and he had to turn the volume on the T.V. pretty loud.

Mum told us we both needed to have a better day tomorrow. She told me not to do anymore Superman's over the couch and gave me a kiss on the head. Then she told dad that being at work was no excuse to wait so long to go to the doctor and gave him a kiss on the head.

Dad's ear didn't hurt very much the next day although he was deaf in his left ear for over a week before his hearing started to come back. Mum sure did get tired of dad not being able to hear her.

I think there was couple of times when she told him about some chores she wanted him to do that he was intentionally ignoring her.

I think she must have suspected the same thing. To make sure he didn't miss anything because of his bad hearing she went to her desk and sat down. She grabbed some paper and a pen and started writing. She gave it to him and he groaned and mumbled about it being a huge honey-do list. She chuckled and headed off to work.

I decided not to do any more dives over the back of the couch and I think mum really appreciated that. When she got home from work she even took me to the glass door in front of the porch to watch the birds fly around. Watching the birds always got me excited and I did a little goose honk at one of them. This always made mum laugh hysterically and her laughs always made me really happy.

Leroy and Amelia figured out that if mum picked me up and took me to the glass door, there would likely be treats soon afterwards. Mum knew I didn't like being held too long so she always made sure that I got treats when she put me down. Grace could smell a treat from anywhere in the house and as soon as treats came out she would come running. Even if she was sound asleep she would jump up to join in. She got two of her treats and a new chew bone.

Watching the birds got me in the mood to play with my feathers and it felt like it took forever for couch time to get there that night. When it was finally that time, I chirped at dad as soon as he sat down to let him know it was time to play. I played for an extra-long time until I got so tired I decided to lie down for a little while and rest. It didn't happen often but every once in a while after playing for a long time I just fall asleep. That's what happened that night. Before I even got my nightly treats I'd fallen asleep.

Chapter Two – The Birdy in the Window

Neuro Dan - Feather Dan

February 14, 2016 ·
Happy Valentine's Day my friends. Today dad went to the mailbox and brought me back so many valentines and toys. Mum sat down and read every one of them to me. There are not enough words to tell you how much I love you. Each and every one of you means so much to me. Sleep with the angels. Love, Dan

It had been a while since it happened but I had an accident one night while I was doing my business. I made it off Blankets Mountain just fine and walked over to my usual spot. I got my business done but I heard Leroy getting into something in the kitchen. I was curious so I tried to jump up onto the top of the cushion to take a look, but I misjudged and slid back down. It was just really bad luck but, I landed in my business. I tried to get some of it off on my way back to Blankets Mountain but I had a feeling I was getting a sink bath in the morning.

I was right. When mum got up she went to get her coffee. When she came back through she stopped to tell me good morning and noticed that the back of both of my legs and part of my tail were a mess. She put her coffee down and left to get a wet washcloth. She tried to clean it up that way but things had dried too much and it wasn't going to come off without some soaking. She told me she was sorry, went to get some towels, and then carried me into the kitchen.

Mum had gotten really good at giving me my sink baths. She didn't even need dad to help anymore; although if he was there, she would recruit him to get it done more quickly. It took a minute to get it done and I made sure to give her plenty of mournful, soul-torn meows in the process. They didn't stop her, but she kept telling me she was sorry until she was finally wrapping me up in a towel to dry me off. She sat down at her desk and gave me luvins to keep me warm while I dried off in the towel.

The previous day gramma had brought over an electric blanket. Mum hadn't had time to open it and set it up yet. Once she set me back on Blankets Mountain so I could work on getting my fur just right again, she disappeared to get it. It only took her a couple of minutes to set it up. She plugged it into the wall beside the couch and laid it out on the couch next to Blankets Mountain. I watched her with intense curiosity while I was cleaning myself up because extra motivation to be good. Plus, gramma always gets really happy after I eat well and that makes me feel happy too.

There was a really bad snow storm that afternoon. Lots of places get snow storms all of the time but we're in North West Georgia and we don't get them often. The storm turned into something mum told me was a blizzard. She canceled work when she heard about the change in the forecast and hurried home so she wouldn't be on the road.

Dad was stuck at work and couldn't leave right away. By the time he left the roads were bad and it took him a long time to get home. Mum kept calling to check on him and make sure he was okay. When he finally walked in the door, he looked pretty relieved. He told mum it was a good thing she got home early because it was really bad out there. He'd even taken one of his employee's home who lived nearby because they were afraid to drive in it. Dad had gone off the road twice and got stuck, but was able to get going again. He said he couldn't even get his truck to our building and had to park all the way at the front of the apartment complex. Then he had to walk the rest of the way home.

When mum and dad sat down for couch time, dad started reading the comments my friends had made from the post mum put up on Facebook earlier. After he finished reading them he started to chuckle and told mum that the troll better not be bold enough to post directly to the page. Mum asked him why and he told her to read the comments because my friends were asking who it was so they could all tell him what they thought about him. Dad told me I might have my own Facebook mafia and those trolls better be careful in the future. Mum read the comments, giggled a little and told dad she agreed with him. Now I am not sure what a Facebook mafia is, but apparently it is a good thing to have.

Dad got a funny look on his face and mum must have been able to read his mind because she told him not to do it. Dad told her the troll would deserve all of the comments my friends would make, but mum told him she didn't want any of my friends getting banned from Facebook. Even if he did deserve it she said that she didn't want any more negativity because of the bully's message.

The next morning mum and dad got up to go to work but when they looked outside they both got on their phones and started making calls. Mum got done first and she said she had canceled all of her clients for the day. Dad took a minute longer but when he hung up he said he wasn't going anywhere either. That meant I got a middle of the week snow day with both mum and dad home! I was super excited and happy because that never happened!

Dad took Grace outside and when he came back in he was trying to get mum to bring a towel. Grace was covered in snow and it was packed between her paws. He wanted to rub it out and get her dried off so she wouldn't get sick and or track all that snow mud through the house. Mum gave him a towel and poked her head outside. She came right back in and said that she had just seen a weather report and it didn't look like anything was going to be melting for at least two days.

They spent most of the day sitting on the couch with me giving me luvins and playing with feathers. Mum got a notion when dad started to take Grace out on one of her bathroom breaks. She decided she was going to take me on a mini adventure and put on her jacket. She scooped me up and we all went outside.

Dad took Grace out into the yard and my ears perked up when I heard the snow crunching under his feet. She took me to the edge of the sidewalk so I could see the snow up close. It was fascinating! I stood up in her arms and sniffed at the big, beautiful snowflakes that were falling down. They felt funny when they melted on my nose and it only took a few seconds before some started to settle on my fur. Mum let me enjoy the experience for a few minutes and when dad came back with Grace we all went back inside.

We came back inside mum and set me down on the electric blanket so I would get warmed back up quickly. Leroy came up and sniffed me. I must have had outside smells on me because he got the same kind of funny look on his face that he did when I came back from the vets. The outside smell must have made him frisky because he got the zoomies and played a game of chase with Amelia. Grace joined in after a few minutes because one of them almost knocked over a lamp. She chased Leroy down, stuck her nose between his back legs, flipped her head and gave him the pit maneuver. Amelia made it to the kitchen counter and got away.

The snow lasted the entire weekend. Neither mum nor dad had to go to work so we all had a great time. Dad walked down to the mail boxes because it had been a while since he checked the mail and mum told him one of my Facebook friends said they had mailed me a surprise. When he got back he had a stack of mail and a package for me!

Mum sat down with me and we opened it up. Inside was a huge Macaw feather! It was yellow with a blue tip and edges. It was almost as long as I was and it had a thick stem that I could tell was going to be perfect for chomping. I stood up and swatted at it. Mum chuckled and set it down for me to play with. I sniffed it for a minute then settled in to give the stem a great big chomp. It made a wonderful crunching noise that got me excited and I chomped it many more times. I chomped on that McCaw feather for a few days. It finally started warming up outside and the snow began to melt. I passed the time enjoying the electric blanket and my new feather. The Macaw feather sure was fun but what happened next was one of the most exciting things I'd experienced.

Mum and dad were both home one evening. I was sitting on top of Blankets Mountain, grooming. Leroy and Amelia had just been fed their lunch so they were on the table eating and Grace was sitting next to dad by his desk. Mum was at her desk working on some reports when we heard a strange commotion outside on the porch.

A chair had been knocked over and bumped into the glass door. Then the table went scooting across the porch into the rails and everything on it hit the floor. Grace got excited and rushed at the door barking loudly. Dad and mum both looked and outside cat DJ was running and jumping everywhere like he'd been stung by a bee. He was racing all over frantically. Everything on the ground was being kicked around and DJ was even trying to climb the walls. Leroy and Amelia had run over to see what was happening and I was standing up trying to see too.

It only took a second to figure out what was going on. A small brown and white bird had managed to get in the small hole in the screen that dad had made so DJ could come in and out. The bird had gotten trapped inside. DJ just happened to come in looking for lunch when he saw the bird hanging on the side of the screen in his porch. DJ always thought of himself as quite the hunter although he rarely ever managed to catch anything. This opportunity was too much for him and he was in full blown zoomies chase mode.

The bird was flying all over the place as fast as it could. It would land on the screen and DJ would jump up and start to climb the screen after it. The bird panicked and flew to another spot but DJ was always right behind it. Grace was barking nonstop and Leroy was front and center with her watching the excitement.

Mum pushed Grace and Leroy back and opened the screen door. Grace tried to lunge out with mum but dad caught her by her collar. Leroy tried to run out and join DJ in the game of chase but dad caught him just in time. Dad told mum to shut the door and when she saw dads predicament she did right away. Dad let Grace go, scooped up Leroy and Amelia and quickly shut them in the bedroom.

Mum was trying to get around DJ but I didn't even think that it registered with him that mum was out there. He was too focused on the bird to notice anything else. Dad grabbed one of my light blankets and was headed to the porch to help mum. She didn't end up needing any help. I watched her put the chair back upright, hop up on it and scoop that little bird off the screen with her hands.

She had it cupped gently in both hands and turned towards the door. DJ couldn't figure out where the bird had gone and was looking everywhere. Grace was still barking and dad bumped her out of the way so he could open the door for mum. She came inside and told dad she'd caught it. He shut the screen door and hurried around her to the front door and opened it for her. Mum walked right past me on Blankets Mountain and I got to see the bird up close. It was just a few inches away from me and at eye level when mum walked by. The poor bird looked scared. Its eyes were wild and it was panting.

Dad followed mum outside. Mum told me that she took the bird around behind some other apartments away from where DJ would be looking. She set it on a branch of a tree and stood there keeping watch over it. It took a few minutes for it to get its senses together; then it flew away. When they came back inside mum went to wash her hands and dad let Leroy and Amelia out of the bedroom. Grace had settled down and was just following dad everywhere he went, trying to heard him towards his desk.

Dad went outside to clean up the disaster that DJ just caused. DJ was still looking around for the bird but at least he wasn't running around with the zoomies. He stayed on the porch and kept looking for it for a long time. He didn't give up his search until later when dad took Grace out. He then left the porch then and followed Grace while she tried to do her business.

I stayed frisky all night long after that. Getting to see the bird so close was a wonderful surprise. It sure did look delicate and I felt bad for it that it got so scared. I was glad mum was able to save it. DJ doesn't know any better I guess, but I think those birds are a lot more fun to watch and I can't imagine they actually taste good either. I will stick to my wet food and treats, thank you very much!

Chapter Three – JuJu

Neuro Dan - Feather Dan

February 3, 2016 ·

Hai my furiends. Iz got another new FEATHER to play with. KT sent me this seagull FEATHER and Iz having a great time with it. It makes fun crunchy noises when I chomps on it. Iz play with this then get Temptations and chin scratches and snuggles! Sleep with the angels my friends Iz love you all.

I was watching Leroy do one of his odd middle of the night patrols when mum surprised me and came out of the bedroom. She was rubbing her eyes and trying to see what was on her phone. She saw me stand up in excitement at seeing her. Anytime she came out of the bedroom and was trying to wake up, I always got excited. I gave her my happy, loving, big-eyed stare. She smiled back and came over to sit down with me. She rubbed my head while she looked at her phone. She grunted and started typing something back then put the phone down.

She turned back to me and told me some people were rude. She said that some people didn't know what appropriate times to message people were. She told me her client had cancelled for that morning so now she'd get to spend the day with me. I gave her lots of wet-face mushes and purred for her. I was pretty sure I could get her to forget about the rude person and get her tired enough to fall back asleep.

She kept rubbing my ears and I figured if she wasn't going to go back to bed right away I might as well get some belly rubs. I rolled over, stretched out and gently touched her arm with my front feet. She laid her head down next to me and started rubbing my belly. She told me that it was going to be a fun week. She said that dad was taking some vacation time at the end of the week. She said he was going to stay at home so I'd get lots of extra luvins and play time.

She rubbed my belly for a little while longer and realized something. She sat up and gave me a great big smile and a happy look. I looked at her upside down, wondering if my belly rubs were going to continue. She told me that she just realized that I was coming up on what she called my gotcha day. It was almost my one year anniversary of being in my forever home.

That brought back a whole bunch of memories. I sat back up and gave mum an inquisitive look. She told me that one year ago today we had never seen each other in person and I was still living at Misfits Critter Farm and Sanctuary. A lot had changed since then and the changes were all for the better. I remembered how scared I was when I had to leave the rescue. I started thinking about JuJu again too. I hadn't heard mum say anything about her or the other kitties at Misfits for a while.

Mum must have been thinking the same thing because she yawned and picked up her laptop. She brought it back to the couch and sat back down with me. She asked me if I wanted to see what had been going on at Misfits. Well of course I did! I started to get really excited. I settled in and got comfortable while she got my Facebook page pulled up. She started reading some of the recent posts to me and I was happy to hear that some of the other cats who were there while I was, had been adopted.

Mum finally got to JuJu's section and we both got a really big surprise. JuJu had been adopted not long ago. I was so happy! JuJu got a forever home! Mum was excited too and she kept on reading through older posts. She was trying to find out information on who adopted her and where she went, but she couldn't find anything. She told me she would ask KT but she wasn't going to be one of those rude people who wake people up in the middle of the night, so I would have to wait until the morning. Mum told me she was getting sleepy, gave me some yummy ear scritches and went back to bed shortly after that.

I was so excited that I stayed up and didn't even snooze for the rest of the night. I decided I had to do something to help pass the time. I wanted the morning to come more than ever so I could find out what happened to JuJu. I decided that I would follow Leroy on one of his patrols the next time he came through. I got down off Blankets Mountain and waited by the cat tree. I gave him quite the surprise when he came around the corner. He wasn't used to seeing me lurking about like that. I gave him the same eager, big-eyed stare I give mum

I knew I wouldn't be able to keep up with him, but I also knew that he went the same way every time. I watched him make a circle through the living room and when he was almost done patrolling that area, I started walking towards the kitchen. Leroy hopped up on top of the couch then dropped off the back and got surprised again when he saw me waiting for him in front of the kitchen.

He gave me a funny look and did a quick stroll through the kitchen. While he did that, I began shuffling down the hall towards the front door and guest bedroom. He finally asked me what I was doing when he saw me heading down the hall. I told him I was going on patrol with him. His eyes narrowed and he let me know that I shouldn't be doing patrols and that I needed to let him and Amelia handle it. He still wouldn't tell me what he was on the lookout for so I kept following him.

He sniffed around the front door and wandered in the guest bedroom. I rarely ever went back there. Mum and dad never went in there and it was always too quiet in there for my taste. The rest of the house felt like it was full of life and energy but the guest room was just dark and quiet. I took a couple of steps in, just enough to be able to watch Leroy wander through the closet and walk to the other side of the bed. He crawled around under the bed and came back out.

He narrowed his eyes and gave me another funny look before he walked into the guest bathroom. I didn't follow him in there because that's where one of the cat boxes was and I thought it would be polite to let him do his business in private if he needed to. I started to make my way back down the hall towards the living room. Leroy came out pretty quick and stopped to give me a few grooming kisses on my head before he trotted back off to the main bedroom.

It took me quite a while and I had almost managed to get back on Blankets Mountain before dad got up. He saw me trying to get up the steps by the couch and came to set me in my bathroom spot. He sure did have good timing with that lately because I had been trying hard not to go on the floor. He took Grace out and then got ready for work. By the time he was ready to go I managed to get back on top of Blankets Mountain. He smiled and stopped to give me some ear rubs before he left. I made sure to give him wet face mushes so he'd have a good day.

When mum got up she went about her morning routine. I was so excited to learn about what happened to JuJu that I couldn't even sit still. I was up and walking circles. Anytime mum looked at me or walked by I stood up and made myself as tall as I could to get her attention. Once she finished her coffee she said she would send KT a message to ask about JuJu. Now I just had to wait for KT to answer. I knew how busy she was every day trying to care for all of the cats at Misfit's so I figured I would have to wait a while longer before I got any answers.

Mum made my breakfast, carried me to my spot on the lower ledge of the cat tree and started feeding me. That is when I realized I was really hungry. All of that extra exercise I got doing that patrol with Leroy gave my appetite a boost. I finished all of my food quickly which made mum happy. It wasn't long and I was back on my spot on Blankets Mountain.

Mum was on the phone with gramma planning to go out to lunch with her and gramma-great. I was starting to think that I was going to have to wait until dinner time or later before I'd get news about JuJu, but mums computer chimed. Mum hung up with gramma and went to check the message. It was a message from KT! Mum started reading and typed something back. She then made her way towards me sat down beside Blankets Mountain. She told me that JuJu got adopted by a young couple who had a little girl. KT told her that the little girl and JuJu bonded right away and she was very relieved that JuJu found a forever home.

I was so happy! It was a dream comes true for me. She even had a little girl to watch out for and play with. JuJu was the best friend ever to me when I was struggling. That little girl had no idea how lucky she was. She would have a best friend to grow up with and make beautiful memories with that she would remember forever. I was a little sad though because mum said she didn't know any other details about the family. I didn't know if JuJu would ever be able to see one of my updates again. I took comfort in knowing that at least she knew I had the best home ever and she would know that I would always be happy.

When mum and dad got home that night they were talking about a bad storm that was going to be coming through. It sounded to me like they were ready for the weather to get a little more stable than it had been. It sounded like it was going to be a loud thunderstorm. Well, this time I wasn't scared. I planned on sleeping right through the night. I was in such a good mood from finding out that JuJu had a forever home that I wasn't worried about any storms or thunder booms.

The next day I got a package in the mail. It was from KT and she sent me a sweet note telling me she was proud of me and that she missed me. She also sent me a great big seagull feather! I didn't waste any time before I started chomping on it. It was a great chomping feather and made wonderful crunching noises.

Before I knew it dad was taking some vacation days. I got an extra surprise and mum was able to take the day off too. They went out for a long time but when they came back they came back with gramma and gramma great. It had been a while since we'd seen gramma great. She had been having more of a hard time getting up and down the stairs to get to our apartment so she wasn't visiting as much.

It was a wonderful visit. As it turned out all of them had gone shopping and one of the places they went was a pet store. Gramma and gramma great got us all kinds of things. We got new treats and Grace got a special bone. We all got new toys too. They got me a special bundle of feathers that hung from a string that was attached to a wand that could do something that dad said was called telescoping. The wand could get longer or shorter by pulling on it which made it so dad could do even more tricks when he was playing with me. I played a lot with that toy and told dad it was like he could make the feathers dance in the air.

Gramma asked mum and dad what they were going to do for the Super Bowl this year. Mum said we'd have lots of good food and snacks. She told gramma they were welcome to come over too if they wanted but they weren't very interested in the game. They said they might watch it for the commercials but that was it. Mum told them she was even going to let me have one of my special beef stick treats that my friend, Judith, from the UK sent me. I didn't have a lot of those so I only got them on special occasions. They were really good and I always liked getting those.

I had a great time for the rest of the weekend and when Super Bowl Sunday got here I had a good time watching mum and dad get ready. They went out to the store and came back with bags of things they were going to cook. I wondered if it was going to start smelling as good as Thanksgiving did. They started cooking a little while after lunch time and they took a couple of hours before they took a break. Mum told dad that they were making an awful lot for just the two of them but that they would have some great snacks and leftovers all week long.

Once the game got started it got pretty rowdy and loud. Mum was rooting for a team called the Panthers and dad was rooting for a team called the Broncos. The more the game went on the more the yelling and cheering went on. I decided I would root for the Panthers with mum because they had pictures of cats on their uniforms.

Mum and dad ate all kinds of food. They had hot wings, cheese dip, sausage balls and different kinds of cheese and crackers. I got my special beef stick and a couple of bites of some cheese that mum liked. I think mum and dad were both pretty full by the time the game was done. Dad's team wound up winning but mum didn't seem to get mad about her team losing. Dad didn't give mum any grief over his team winning. They were both rooting for teams but neither of the teams were their favorite teams.

I wondered if JuJu and her new family had been watching the game. Dad said that a lot of people watched it every year and that it was a kind of celebration. I thought it sounded like another tradition that people had. It gave them a reason to come together and celebrate for no real reason at all. I thought that was wonderful. People could come up with some pretty creative ways to find reasons to get together. I enjoyed it any time there was a reason to come together and do something. They had fun and so did I.

Chapter Four – Gotcha Day Celebration

Neuro Dan - Feather Dan

February 14, 2016 ·

Happy Valentine's Day my friends. Today dad went to the mailbox and brought me back so many valentines and toys. Mum sat down and read every one of them to me. There are not enough words to tell you how much I love you. Each and every one of you means so much to me. Sleep with the angels. Love, Dan

Mum had been talking to dad about a cold front that was moving in for a few days. It finally got here. It came in quickly overnight and dropped the temperatures very rapidly. I didn't respond well to it. Now and then my neurological condition would act up when there was a sudden change in weather and this time, for no reason I could tell, it hit me harder than normal.

I was having a very difficult time moving. I'd keep telling my feet what to do and they only did about half of what they should have. My front feet and back feet weren't coordinating like I was trying to make them. My head was doing its wobbly thing on me and I was struggling to keep my balance. The entire situation wasn't just overwhelmingly frustrating; it was physically exhausting as well.

I'd experienced this before when there were drastic changes in the weather so I kind of understood what was happening but I couldn't help but to be scared. Mum called the vet and talked to him. He told her there was nothing that we could do about it except to keep me warm and as comfortable as possible. Mum said keeping me warm would be easy with the electric blanket.

She tried to feed me my breakfast but I struggled to hold my head steady and I couldn't get comfortable. She kept trying to get me to eat for over an hour and a half, but I barely ate anything. When I did try to get a bite most of it would fall out of my mouth and make a mess on my chest and legs. I dropped a lot of food over the edge of my shelf but Grace was right there and quick to help get it cleaned up. I finally had enough of it and tried to get up to turn around. I got stuck but mum saw what was happening and she gathered me up.

She carried me to my bathroom spot on the couch and stood there until I was done. She made sure she scooped me up and set me on Blankets Mountain before I would do anything that would require a sink bath. She cleaned up the couch, changed out blankets and pads. When she went to get the rest of my food off the plate she had set on the floor by my ledge she noticed it was gone. Grace was looking terribly guilty and snuck away into the bedroom. Mum picked up that mess too, then came and sat down with me.

She stroked my head and rubbed my ears. She told me I'd be okay and hoped that the spell would pass quickly. It was supposed to stay really cold for several days. She told me we'd keep it extra warm inside and I could just get some rest on the electric blanket. She set up some extra blankets around the top of Blankets Mountain to act as a small barrier to help keep me from falling off. She knew me well enough to know that even when I don't feel good, I'm likely to get a notion. She knew I'm stubborn enough to fight through things and get adventurous anyway. I didn't think she had to worry about that this time. I really didn't want to do anything except go to sleep and hope I woke up feeling better.

She went to work and I slept the entire day until dad got home. Mum let him know I wasn't feeling good so as soon as he took Grace out for her walk he came right over to see me. He gave me luvins for a while and talked to me. He quickly noticed that I was not feeling very good. He told me how much he wanted me to feel better and said he was going to try to find some ways to help. I wasn't sure how he was going to do that, but he was dad and he always surprised me with how he found ways to make life easier, so I would wait and see.

He made my dinner and took me to my ledge to feed me. I didn't have any more luck trying to eat with him than I did with mum. Grace was enjoying all of the wet food I was dropping off the back of the ledge. Leroy and Amelia figured out that I was dropping food and they decided to join Grace. It became a little free for all at the bottom of the cat tree while they all raced to see who could get to the dropped food fastest. In fact, Amelia kept her head directly under me and would sometimes end up with a mouthful on her head. When Grace figured out this was happening, she decided that Amelia's head was a free for all too.

Dad then did the same thing that mum did and took me to my bathroom spot. He watched over me until I was done with my business and quickly got me to the heated blanket on top of Blankets Mountain. He got things cleaned up and told me he would come up with something to get me some fluids. He always listened to mum and knew that was going to be what worried her the most so he was already working on a solution.

When mum and dad sat down that night for couch time, mum let all of my friends know I wasn't feeling well. She didn't even have to ask them for prayers. They all sent me so much love, prayers and well wishes that I couldn't see how this could last too long. Just like he said he would, dad got an idea and went over to mums desk. He dug around in the treat drawer for a minute. That got Leroy, Amelia and Grace to run out from other rooms in the apartment to make sure they wouldn't miss anything good.

He found what he was looking for and when he turned around, he realized that he had a small audience sitting patiently behind him. He sighed and got Grace a bone. Then he grabbed a bag of Temptations and gave it to mum to share with Leroy and Amelia. He walked into the kitchen and when he came back, he had a plastic spoon. He'd found some of my treats that were a thick liquid. Mum and dad thought it smelled weird but I really liked it. It was a creamy tuna-flavored yogurt sauce that really hit the spot for me.

He squirted some on the spoon and held it under my nose for me. I didn't even have to try to coordinate my neck muscles to get it. All I had to do was lick it up and eat it that way. I got three packs of that yummy stuff before mum told dad to quit or I'd probably end up needing a sink bath in the morning. Mum told him that was a good idea and at least that got me some fluids for the night. She said she would stop at the pet store in the morning and try to find something that would be easier for me to eat until I started feeling better.

The next day, mum brought home some new food for me to try at lunch. It was wet food but all natural with chunks of yummy salmon. She set me on my ledge and used tiny pieces of the salmon to hand fed me. I didn't have to try to hold my head or take bites and keep it in my mouth so I was able to eat some. She also put some of the liquid from the can on the spoon and let me lick it up like I did with what dad had fed me the night before. It felt good to get some food in me but not as good as mum and dad made me feel. They always tried so hard to take care of me. I always appreciated everything they did because I knew that I took quite a bit of time to care for.

By the time mum was done feeding me we both felt better. My stomach was full and I wasn't thirsty. Mum wasn't nearly as worried about me getting dehydrated or sitting around all day hungry. I made sure to purr loudly and give her extra kisses. She helped me take care of my bathroom ritual and lifted me up on top of Blankets Mountain again. Then she sat down with me and gave me some luvins while she called dad. She told dad how she was able to get met to eat and let him know where she put the special food so he could take care of me when he got home from work.

Dad followed mums instructions to the letter and I was able to get a decent dinner as well. The food was helping me feel a little better, but I was still having a tough time getting my legs to coordinate, so moving wasn't fun at all. Even though it was still hard to be coordinated I was getting bored with just sitting there and I decided I was going to play with some feathers anyway.

Dad played a game with me on Blankets Mountain where he would pop some feathers up from the back of the couch and pull them down quickly. I didn't have to move but I could swat at the feathers when they popped up. I'm pretty sure he let me catch a few but I still had fun and even did some good feather chomping. After that, I stayed curled up on top of Blankets Mountain enjoying the electric blanket.

Mum read the comments from the post the night before and she realized something. She realized that I had gotten a lot more Facebook fans. They understood that I had a disability but they didn't know what it was or the details of it. Mum decided that it was time to share my story with everyone again. That's what she did with my Facebook post that night. She had plenty of people thank her for the information and it took her most of the night to respond and make sure everyone knew I wasn't in pain and that I was happy and loving life. I always thought it was sweet how people would care for and worry about me. It made me feel special and it warmed my heart.

That nasty cold front stuck around for a few more days. I started getting a little bit better every day and that made mum feel better. She was still worried that this episode would result in a permanent progression of my disease and cause me to have increased difficulty moving around. I wanted to tell her not to worry, but it wouldn't have done any good. Mum loved me so much that she would worry about everything no matter what I said to her. I wasn't worried though. I didn't feel like anything was going to be a permanent set back. Sometimes you just know that things will be okay and in that instance I knew I was going to bounce back quickly.

I was able to eat better with each day that went by. I got control of my neck muscles again and was able to take bites off of the food mum piled up on my plate. Leroy, Amelia and Grace were a bit disappointed when I stopped dropping food all over the floor. Grace even tried to sniff my belly to see if I had dropped any food there but that got her fussed at by mum.

I always believe you should look for the positive in any situation. It really doesn't do any good to just dwell on the bad stuff. Doing that only keeps you feeling bad. In this instance, I thought that it was funny that my neurological episode created a new tradition. From that point forward when I got my breakfast and dinner it became a family event.

Leroy, Amelia and Grace would all gather around my bottom ledge of the cat tree and wait to see if I would drop any food. I thought it was fun and sometimes, just because I wanted to share, I would make sure to drop some food for them on purpose. Sometimes I would even shake my head and the food would go flying. Mum and dad didn't like it when I did that because every now and then it would stick to the wall and Grace would lick the spot for five minutes before she'd quit.

Once the cold front was gone I was completely back to my old self. I felt wonderful and made sure dad knew about it by letting him know I was playful. Mum told me that she was extremely happy that I felt perfect because that day was my official gotcha day! She said that it was one year ago that day that Ken carried me through the front door and set me down on the dining room floor.

That brought back lots of memories and mum and dad were sharing stories of how hard it had seemed to get me figured out in the beginning. Now they couldn't imagine life without me and they laughed when they remembered all of the challenges that frustrated them in the beginning. It reminded me of how lucky I was and how loved I was. I had the best home and family I could have ever even dreamed of.

All of the memories they were sharing and all of the laughter made me frisky, so I gave dad a big honk to let him know it was time to play. We played feathers hard that night. I was back to leaping after the feathers that dad would make dance on top of the couch and I was jumping higher than usual to get to them. I had to make up for lost play time and the extra play time seemed like it made dad happy too. The extra high jumps were making mum laugh and for a while, we all forgot about how I had been feeling so sick over the last week.

We also got extra messages from my Facebook friends that night. Lots of people told mum to be sure to check the mail the next day. Dad told me that it was going to be Valentine's Day in just two days. Dad reminded me about how we couldn't let on to mum that we would be doing something special for her, but he assured me we would be. I'm pretty sure mum knew that dad was playing dumb but she didn't say anything.

The next day when dad came home from work he had all kinds of extra shopping bags and packages with him. He told me it was a good thing he was able to check the mail before mum did because her surprises had shown up. We both knew if she saw the packages addressed to dad at this time of year, she would have been quick to open them so she wouldn't be surprised. He looked at the clock and told me he didn't have much time before she got home so we'd have to hurry. He hid a package by his desk and quickly took Grace out for her walk. When he came back he got some wrapping paper and got her package all wrapped up. He showed me the cards he got for her and told me one of them would be from me, Leroy, Amelia and Grace. I thought that was a great idea because she always got the biggest smile on her face when she got a card from us.

He got the packages and cards hidden away just in time. He had just walked back into the living room to pick up the wrapping paper and put it away when the front door opened and mum walked in. He moved pretty quick and kicked the wrapping paper under the couch right before mum walked into the living room. She gave him a funny look but he waved his hands in front of his nose and told her I had just farted. Sure dad, just blame it on the cat!

I turned and gave dad a funny look. I did not fart and that made mum take a step back instead of coming to give me my after-work hello. She decided to go to the kitchen to get a drink and dad winked at me once her back was turned. He scanned the room to make sure there wasn't anything that would give away that he'd just wrapped her presents. He told her I had gotten a lot of mail and she came back out to see.

She stopped and gave me my hello luvins on her way by. She told dad it didn't smell like I farted and he told her that maybe it had been Leroy. Dad was stretching now because Leroy was taking a nap in the bedroom. He was lucky though because mum was curious about what I got in the mail and she went over to take a look. She sat down with me and started opening them up. I got lots of Valentine's Day cards. Mum read them to me and they all had the sweetest messages in them. Mum set them up all over the counters and desks and told me I could enjoy looking at them.

The next day was a lot of fun. Dad got up early and set up mum's desk with her cards and presents just like he always did. She always seemed to get surprised when she saw what was there. I couldn't figure out if she forgot about the holiday or if dad used to forget to do things and she wasn't used to it. I guessed that she just hadn't had her coffee yet and she forgot because dad never seemed to miss a chance to put surprises on her desk.

Mum beat dad home from work that day and she came in loaded up with stuff. I got even more mail including some packages. She sat down with me and read all of the cards to me again. Some of the cards had feathers in them too! She opened my packages for me and I had more treats, toys and something different. One of my friends sent me a heated cat bed. I didn't even know that those existed but I was intrigued at the concept.

Dad got home while mum was opening up my packages. He took the heated cat bed, plugged it in and once it was warm he set me in it. I really liked that! It was soft and had a comfortable place for me to lay my head down. Dad got excited and said he had an idea. He picked me up, set me back on Blankets Mountain and took the cat bed. He carried it over to the glass door, pulled the cord around behind his desk and plugged it in there. Then he came back over, picked me up and carried me over to it. He sat down with me and set me in it and looked over to mum. Mum had a big smile on her face and they could both tell how much I was going to enjoy that.

They were right and again one of dad's ideas was a huge hit for me. I now had two places where I could sit and stay toasty warm. I loved being able to sit in front of the glass door. It was someplace I would spend lots of time in the warmer weather. I didn't spend very much time looking outside during the winter because I could feel the cold through the door and it would make me uncomfortable. Now I could sit there and be warm while I enjoyed my view outside.

I got to spend the rest of the winter wandering back and forth between Blankets Mountain and the glass door. It wound up being a great bonus for Leroy and Amelia too. As soon as I started spending time in front of the glass door they both discovered the heating pad on top of Blankets Mountain. They decided they liked it as much as I did. Then when I went back to Blankets Mountain, they discovered the heated cat bed and they loved that too.

There were many times that I would just sit and think. I would wonder about things a lot. I'd wonder how KT was doing and if JuJu was having as good of a life as I was. I wondered about how many other traditions there were that I didn't know about yet. By the end of February, I really was just wondering how much better my life could be and if it was even possible to be happier than I was then. I loved my life. It was an incredible journey filled with the most amazing experiences and I woke up each day eager to see what would happen next.

Chapter Five – To the Top of the World

Neuro Dan - Feather Dan

April 13, 2016 ·

Hai my furiends. Iz seeing if I can get mum to go get those yummy special beef stick treats out of her desk drawer. I know right where they are. They are in the top right drawer so she doesn't even have to look for them I've kept a close eye on that drawer. Please? Maybe my friends can help convince her. I know it's not a special occasion but I like them so much! Sleep with the angels my friends. I luvs you all.

A few days' later mum and dad came home from a dinner date. When they walked inside they were reading a letter that had been taped to the front door. Mum was saying that she didn't like it and wasn't sure what they were supposed to do with me while that was happening. Dad grabbed Grace's leash and told her they would figure something out. He took Grace out for her walk and mum got on her phone to call gramma.

She sat down next to me while she talked to gramma and gave me chin scritches. Mum told gramma that the apartment complex was going to be doing some pretty significant work on the buildings. She mentioned something about upgrading pipes and plumbing systems. It turned out our apartment was one of the ones they were going to need access to. They were going to be cutting open the ceiling to get to the pipes and they needed all kinds of prep work to be done ahead of time.

Dad came back in, picked up the letter, stood in the center of the living room and started looking at the ceiling. It didn't take long and he was grumbling up a storm. He pointed to the ceiling right above his desk and continued to point and moves his hand from his desk all the way down the wall towards the kitchen. He was pretty grumpy too. He told mum the apartment complex expected them to be able to clear everything several feet away from the wall through that entire path.

Mum looked at the ceiling and said a bad word. Dad said that it would have been nice to have more than a couple of hours' notice. They were going to have to move not only dad's desk that had a lot of stuff on it but the entertainment center with the television as well as the cat tree. Dad looked at mum and asked her if she had any idea where they were supposed to put all of that stuff. She started getting irritated too when she realized exactly what it was they were going to have to do.

At that point, I was perked up and very interested. This sounded like the makings of an excellent adventure. I knew mum and dad were not happy about being surprised with having to get a lot done on short notice, but I thought it would be very entertaining to watch. Dad sat down at his desk and started pulling things off and carrying them into the bedroom.

Mum went into the kitchen and got my dinner ready. She then carried me to the cat tree and set me on my ledge. She told dad she wanted to get me fed before we started doing too much because she was worried that all of the commotion would distract me and I wouldn't eat well. Dad agreed and decided to go get his work things ready for the next day instead of moving things around in the living room. He knew if there was a lot of commotion going on, I would get distracted from eating.

He told mum that they also wanted the laundry closet emptied out. He told her they were on their own with that one because he wasn't dragging the washing machine and dryer anywhere. He cleared everything off the shelf in the laundry closet while mum finished feeding me. After mum got me settled back on Blankets Mountain, they teamed up to getting the work done.

I watched them work and I couldn't have been more entertained. Everything was getting put right in the middle of the living room. Dad pushed the coffee table all the way over to mums desk and they dragged the entertainment center right up in front of the couch. There were cords all over the place. The internet stuff was all set up on dad's desk and his desk is an old sectional desk that mum always says looks like it would fall over if it wasn't up against a wall. Dad never disagreed with her and it looked like we were all going to see just how sturdy it would be. It wound up in the middle of the living room with everything else. I had to admit it looked a bit wobbly but it didn't fall over.

The cat tree got pushed right up beside Blankets Mountain. I thought that was wonderful! The tube part that is above the ledge I eat on was level with part of Blankets Mountain and I could walk right off the couch and onto it. I had big plans for that tonight. Amelia was sitting up on the very top of mum's desk watching everything. When she saw where the cat tree wound up she hopped down to go check it out.

She hopped up into the tube part. She sniffed, looked around and when she saw me she gave me one of her sassy hisses. Then she jumped up through the hole in the top of it and climbed up to the next ledge where mum kept most of our toys when we weren't playing with them. One more hop and she was all the way up on the top looking over the rearranged living room.

It took them a minute to get everything done and it was after eight o'clock when they finally finished. They took turns getting a shower and then finally sat on the couch. Neither of them was happy with how close the television was and mum asked dad what he thought we should do with me tomorrow. Dad asked mum if she talked to gramma and mum told him she said she could bring me over there if we wanted to. Mum wasn't sure which would be more stressful for me; staying in the apartment with a bunch of loud work and strangers or going to spend the day someplace different. Dad said he thought it would be less stressful at grammas because he knew Grace would spend the entire day locked in the bedroom barking at the workers.

Mum agreed and it was decided. I was going to go for a day trip to grammas tomorrow. Part of me thought that it would be fun. I knew I would also get to see gramma-great and I really enjoyed the times I got to see her. Part of me was also really nervous. Gramma has three kitties of her own and one of them, a tortie, has a reputation for being ugly to new things. The other two sounds really nice but I'd heard gramma talking before and one of them was a really big guy. Not Leroy big either, but big eater big.

At least I wasn't going to the vets. I knew better than to worry about it. Worrying never helped so instead, I spent the evening playing feathers with dad and getting some treats from mum. I was also keeping an eye on the cat tree. I didn't think that I'd let on to mum that I had already gotten a notion about adventuring onto it tonight.

I gave mum and dad an hour to get solidly asleep before I made my move towards the cat tree. I was right; I could step right off of Blankets Mountain and onto the tube. I looked around and over the lip towards the ground. It was fun to be able to see things from a different point of view and I enjoyed seeing my eating ledge from above. I looked up and decided I was going to try to get up to the hole and try to climb even higher.

I studied the hole and the rest of the cat tree for a minute. It was going to be quite the challenge. The hole was pretty high up there for me. I could get up on my back legs but reaching with my front legs would be painful. I walked back and forth and looked at the edges on either side of the tree. I decided that instead of trying to go up through the hole I would go around the side.

I got my claws hooked where I wanted to and did a little hop. I got my back claws hooked in and started pushing myself up. I wasn't stretching my front legs out too far but using them to do little quick steps up. I got to a point where I could wedge my back against the big trunk of the tree and kept on going.

Before I knew it, I was over the lip of the next ledge. I scrambled in and hunkered down so I could get my bearings. There were cat toys everywhere. I was sitting on a pile of them. There were small mouse toys, little funny shaped balls, jingly toys, long fuzzy toys and stuff I'd never even seen. As I kept on looking I found one of my feathers!

Either Leroy or Amelia had taken off with one of my Feathers! I was just beside myself. I kept on poking through the pile of toys but didn't see any more feathers. I took the feather they had taken off with and tossed it off the cat tree. I watched it float down and land on Blankets Mountain. Once I was satisfied that I had recovered my feather and that there were no more I decided I had to take advantage of being so high and check out the very top ledge.

The top ledge wasn't too far above the one I was on. I looked up at it and stood up on my back legs. I rested my front feet on the top ledge and looked at it. There wasn't anything on it. At least they didn't hide any of my feathers up there. I really wanted to get all the way to the top but I knew if I wasn't careful I'd fall off. I looked down realized that if I did fall at least I would land on Blankets Mountain.

There wasn't going to be a better opportunity for me to try. I got up on my back legs again and put my front feet on the top. I crouched and did one of my mightiest leaps ever! I launched up and landed right perfectly on the very top ledge. I hunkered down again for a minute to let my muscles rest and to get my bearings again. When I stood up and looked around I was fascinated. The entire world looked different up here. I was up so high that I would be taller than dad! If he came out he would have to look up to see me.

I was very proud of myself. Despite my disabilities, I managed to go someplace that no one, not even mum or dad, would believe I would ever be able to get to. I did it by myself with no help at all. I couldn't wait for someone to come out so I could show off my accomplishment.

Leroy was the first one to come out. He was out to do his first patrol of the night. He wandered out of the bedroom and started circling around the living room. He sniffed around at the glass door, wandered behind mums desk then hopped up onto the couch. He looked over at Blankets Mountain and didn't see me. He stopped and blinked a few times and looked around. He looked around the floor where dad's desk had been dragged to and checked out the entertainment center. He jumped back up on the couch and climbed up to the top of Blankets Mountain. He sniffed around for a minute but he still didn't see me.

I was peeking down at him from the top ledge. My eyes were wide and bright, my whiskers were flexed with excitement. He was stumped, but I was so excited I accidentally let out a little goose honk. He looked up and saw me. His jaw dropped open and his eyes went wide. He jumped up to the ledge right below me, stood up and looked right at me. He couldn't believe I'd gotten myself up there! Then he asked if I had figured out how I was going to get down yet. I told him nope but I would figure it out one way or another. He gave me a quick lick on the forehead, jumped down to Blankets Mountain and resumed his patrol.

Amelia came out next. She found me pretty quick, but that's only because she went straight to the cat tree and climbed all the way to the top as soon as she came in. She almost fell off the cat tree when she saw me. When she tried to hop up to the top shelf, there I was looking right at her. She lost her balance, staggered and plopped down onto the next ledge. She then stood up and glared at me. She gave me a nasty hiss, promptly turned around and ran off.

Another couple of hours went by and I was starting to think of ways I could get down. I hadn't thought about what I was going to do if I had to go to the bathroom and I didn't think I was going to be able to hold it much longer. I had gotten pretty good at backing myself off my bottom ledge. I was studying the ledge below me and knew it would be easy to back off onto it. I thought that if I did, I could pretty much ease back up and drop down to the tube. Then I could drop down through the hole in the top. I wouldn't even need to figure out how to get down to my bottom ledge I would be able to just walk right back out onto Blankets Mountain.

I was about to put my plans in motion when I saw mum come out of the bedroom and head towards the kitchen. She was pretty sleepy and since she wasn't grumbling at her phone I figured she was just coming out for a quick drink of water. I was right. She walked past Blankets Mountain, went in the kitchen and came out with a glass of water.

When she came back around into the living room I stood up tall and stretched my back. She saw the movement and looked up. When she saw me she stopped dead in her tracks and almost dropped her glass of water. She looked at me and blinked a couple of times. I think she was trying to make sure it was actually me and not Leroy. She looked at Blankets Mountain and back up to me and started talking fast.

She was fussing at me, telling me to be careful, and asking me how I managed to get up there all at the same time. She set down her glass of water and hurried over to me. She stood on the couch right next to Blankets Mountain so she could look at me. I could tell she was worried but mum tended to worry more than I thought she should. I was giving her my biggest "look what I did" smile. She could tell I was quite proud of myself and she stopped fussing at me right away.

She told me she loved me and reached up, took me off of the ledge and gave me a big kiss on my forehead. She held onto me for a minute and she stepped off of the couch. She must have realized I needed to use the bathroom because she set me on my bathroom spot instead of on top of Blankets Mountain. I did my business real quick and she picked me up again. This time she set me down on Blankets Mountain. She sat down with me and talked to me for quite a while. She told me to be more careful and before she went to bed, she dragged the cat tree back up against the wall where it usually was. I had satisfied my notion and hadn't planned on going back up the cat tree anyway so I didn't mind much.

Dad was super impressed about my adventure and accomplishment. Mum told him first thing in the morning as soon as he got back from taking Grace out for a walk. Mum was still a bit exasperated about finding me like that. Dad laughed really loud and asked her how long it took her to figure out it was me. She laughed too and said it took a minute because she didn't believe I could even get up there. They both got a good chuckle out of the shenanigans and agreed that I could never be underestimated.

Chapter Six – Furiends

=

Neuro Dan - Feather Dan March 10, 2016 ·

Darn it mum you are not supposed to be giving me sink baths in front of my gramma! Jeeze she hasn't even been here a day yet. Well anyway I'm gunna be sure I gets extra treats out of this. Now let's play with FEATHERS please! Sleep with the angels my friends. I luvs you.

I had so much fun that night playing on the cat tree that I completely forgot I had to go to grammas. Dad left for work first and mum called gramma while she was getting ready. They talked for a bit and mum went into the guest bedroom. She came out with my cat carrier. She gathered a few of my favorite feathers and a couple of my small soft blankets and put them inside. She set the carrier on the floor and then went about making my breakfast.

Leroy decided he needed to check out my cat carrier. He can never resist getting in a box or anything else that he can stick his head in. He poked around and even though he's super big he managed to get turned around. By the time mum came back with my breakfast he was sitting in it with his head sticking out. Mum laughed at him while she carried me to my ledge on the cat tree. Leroy decided to come out of my carrier when I started eating. He was hoping I'd drop him a snack or two (which of course I did).

Once my breakfast was done and mum let me take care of my business she slid me into my carrier. We went out the door and up the stairs. It was a pretty short walk to get to grammas. Mum left the front flap of my carrier open so I could look around. I was very curious about everything and I thought it would be nice if mum took me on more walks. I usually wound up going to the vet when I got put in my carrier but this was much more fun.

Gramma and gramma-great were both waiting for me when we got there. Mum carried me in and set me down on the coffee table in the living room. Gramma great was extra excited to see me and gave me lots of ear rubs right away. Gramma came over and said hi and mum told her she didn't have much time before she had to leave. She talked to gramma for a few minutes, gave me a kiss on the head, and then out the door she went.

Grammas apartment was designed exactly the same as ours so it felt familiar in an odd way. At least the walls were the same but their furniture was all backwards from what I was used to. The biggest thing that I wasn't sure about was all of the different smells. I knew there were three other cats there. I could smell each one of them. It reminded me of being back at Misfits Critter Farm where there were new cat smells all the time.

Gramma tock me out of my carrier and set me on a nice Sherpa blanket she had on her couch. She let me sit down, sniff for a minute and get comfortable. Then she got out a bag of treats and as soon as she opened it the other three cats came running into the living room. I stood up and studied the situation intensely.

The first cat was an orange cat like me but he was the fattest cat I'd ever seen in my life. He had a huge belly and it swung back and forth under him as he trotted into the room. His body was so big that his head looked too small for his body and his legs looked just a bit short. The next cat that came around from near the back bedroom was another orange but she was much smaller and younger than the big guy. Then, from out of the main bedroom came an old tortie. She was thin, had bits of gray on her fur and looked like she had been around for a long time.

They all ran up to gramma but as soon as they saw me they stopped in their tracks. The tortie was the first one to hiss and she had a hiss that meant business. I gave her my big, wide eyed stare to try to let her know I wasn't a threat but she glared at me and hissed again. Then the big guy hissed at me and that made the orange girl run away back down the hall.

Gramma and gramma- great both fussed at the cats that had hissed and told them to cut it out. The big guy kept an eye on me but it was obvious he wasn't going to let me keep from getting some treats. He walked up to gramma and she gave him a treat then gave me a treat. The big guys name was Paddy. I watched gramma pet him on the head and give him another treat. She looked at the tortie and called for her to come get one too. Her name was Meghan and she just stood there glaring at me.

I was beginning to wonder if all of the female cats in Georgia had such bad attitudes. JuJu was a girl kitty and she liked me just fine. JuJu had never hissed at me, not even once. Meghan growled a very mean sounding growl as I sat down on the blanket. I thought maybe if I ignored her she would just ignore me too and that would be fine by me.

Paddy was rubbing up against grammas leg and making his tail quiver. I knew he was begging for more treats but gramma kept talking to Meghan. She tried one more time to get Meghan to come get a treat but she just turned around and went back into the bedroom. I could tell I'd need to keep a careful eye on her; those growls were serious warnings from her. I had no intention of going anywhere or even getting off of the Sherpa until mum came back to get me. I just hoped that I hadn't been set down on anyone's favorite spot.

Gramma-great came out, got a couple of treats and took them back to the other bedroom for Star to enjoy. Gramma-great came out and sat in a rocking chair in the living room while gramma stayed on the couch with me. Paddy wandered around a bit and when he realized he wasn't getting anymore treats, he wandered over to see if there was any food in the food bowl.

We sat like that for most of the day. Paddy came over a few times. He hopped up and checked me out from the top of the couch once, but when I looked up at him he hissed. Gramma then fussed at him and shewed him away. Meghan came back out a few times. She always stopped at the entrance to the bedroom and hissed at me, then went about her business. We kept to ourselves. Star finally came back out and I watched her and Paddy play with some mouse toys.

The play looked like it was lots of fun but I wasn't about to get off my spot on the couch. I wasn't pushing my luck with Meghan at all. After Paddy and Star started to play, he quit hissing at me. After a while, both he and Star came up to me and sniffed noses.

Gramma stayed with me all day and if she even walked off for just a minute she had gramma-great come sit with me.

Dad got home from work before mum did so he came over and got me right away. Gramma told him all about how my day went and let him know I didn't even take one nap. She was right, I knew better than to doze off unless the other cats were more used to me. Dad said he'd get me home, give me my dinner and see if I wanted to play or nap. I wasn't in the mood for anything but to just go home but I figured I'd do both play and nap before the night was over.

It had started to rain just as he started to walk me back home. When he got about halfway there it started to pour heavy. He moved pretty quickly when it did that, and I thought that the run in the rain was really fun and exciting. I stayed nice and dry in my carrier but he was drenched and his clothes were soaked. He set my carrier down on the floor and got me out. He dripped water all over me when he pulled me out and it tickled a little, but he set me on Blankets Mountain and it felt wonderful to be home again.

Dad opened up the bedroom door to let Grace, Leroy and Amelia out and right away Grace was hopping up and down and whining at him. She had to go out for her walk really badly. Dad looked at her, grabbed her leash and looked around for an umbrella. Mum must have taken the umbrella with her that morning because he groaned, shook his head and walked out with Grace. When he came back in both him and Grace were dripping wet messes. He grabbed a towel and tried to get Grace dried off but she was shaking hard and sending water all over the hallway.

Dad took his shoes off there, let Grace off her leash and went back to grab a shower and get in some dry clothes. Mum came home while he was in the shower and she sat down to see how I was doing. She had already talked to gramma so she knew how my day had gone. I gave her lots of wet face mushes and purred. When dad came back out he let her know he hadn't had time to feed me yet so she got up and started making my dinner.

Dad grabbed a letter off the kitchen counter and read it to mum. He told her the workers had finished the plumbing work but that they were coming back again tomorrow to fix the holes in the ceiling. I looked up and sure enough there were several holes in the ceiling. Amelia had already climbed up on the cat tree and was trying to see if she could get in one of them. Dad pulled the cat tree farther away so it was out of her reach but mum made him move it more so it wasn't close enough for me to climb on so easily again.

Mum fed me dinner and when she was done she called gramma. She told gramma the plumbers were coming back and that I'd need to spend tomorrow with her again. It sounded like gramma was excited about that, but I wasn't so thrilled. I wondered if I could get mum to send some more feathers with me so I could share them with Paddy, Star and Meghan. If I did this, maybe they wouldn't hiss at me next time.

I played feathers with dad a little that night but not having taken any naps was catching up with me. I wound up falling asleep earlier than normal. I woke up about the time they were going to bed but at least that got me some more luvins before I fell back to sleep on Blankets Mountain. I was still pretty tired and since I was going to be spending the day at grammas again, I decided to just go back to sleep so I'd be rested up.

When mum dropped me off at grammas the next day she was running late and didn't even have time to come in with me. Gramma and gramma-great took me to the same spot on their couch. They still had the Sherpa blanket that I liked laid out for me to sit on. Gramma-great got the treats out and that got Paddy, Star and Meghan running over. They saw me on the couch but this time nobody hissed. We all enjoyed our treats and the other cats wandered back to wherever they had been before I got there.

I thought about it for a minute and was surprised that I didn't seem to bother anyone. I wasn't sure what was different about today than yesterday, but I really appreciated not being hissed at. Gramma sat with me all day. She played feathers with me and when she did Paddy came out and played with me. I enjoyed that quite a bit!

Paddy was a big guy but he knew how to play gentle. Once he came out and played it wasn't long before Star came out to play too. They had fun playing zoomies and when they raced over the back of the couch it surprised me and I hopped up and did one of my goose honks. Gramma got a good laugh out of my goose honk.

The day went by much better than yesterday. I even got comfortable enough to take a nap. Gramma called mum and let her know how well things were going and it sounded like that made mum happy. When dad got home and came over to get me, he was surprised to hear how well we had all gotten along. He put me in my carrier and walked me back to our apartment. It was chilly but nice outside and I enjoyed the walk.

The first thing I looked for when we got inside was to see if the holes in the ceiling had been fixed. There were no holes and the ceiling looked just like it did before they cut it up. Dad read a letter they left on the kitchen counter and he told me the workers were all done and I wouldn't have to go back to grammas tomorrow. I had been looking forward to another day trip to grammas. I was making new friends and it was nice to have gramma sit with me and pay attention to me all day.

Dad was busy pushing all of the furniture back where it belonged when mum got home. She told him how much fun I'd had at grammas and he seemed pretty happy about that. Mum helped him finish getting the living room organized again then went and made my dinner. I played hard with my feathers that night. When I went to sleep, I was happy knowing that I'd made new friends and that I had a spot on grammas couch if I ever needed it.

Chapter Seven – Grammy Visits, Indignant Baths and Nail Trims

Neuro Dan - Feather Dan

March 15, 2016 ·

Hai my furiends. Today gramma brought over one of her kitties so mum could help trim nails and such. Now Iz know the nail trims aren't much fun and itz our sworn duty as cats to protest such things but whoo wee, grammas kitty gets MAD and LOUD. Poor Leroy ran to the other side of the house and got there in a hurry. Mum sayz he's a lover not a fighter. Me and Amelia stayed on the couch and guarded the FEATHERS and treats. Sleep with the angels my friends I loves you all.

The next day I found out two different things. The first thing I heard mum and dad talking about was that my grammy from South Carolina was going to be coming for a visit in just a couple of weeks. That made me happy! The last time she came I got to show her lots of my feather pouncing moves and how potent my surprises could be. I was going to have to think about some new tricks to show her on the next visit. Maybe I'd show her how good I walk across the back of the couch and how nervous it makes mum.

The second thing I heard them talking about was that mum was getting ready to go out of town this weekend. She was going to visit her friend Patti who she met and became good friends with because of me and my Facebook page. Every time mum talks about Patti I feel pretty good that I was able to help her make such a special friend.

Dad planned on staying home with me. He sat down with me and asked me what I'd like to do while mum was gone. He told me it would be a bachelor pad with no mum supervision so we could eat whatever we wanted and play feathers all night. I wasn't real sure what a bachelor pad was but it was sounding pretty fun. He told me all we'd have to do is make sure we got the house cleaned up before mum got home or we'd be in trouble. Well, I would definitely make sure my feathers were picked up so I wouldn't be in trouble; that was for sure.

The weekend got here quickly and the next thing I knew mum was giving me lots of kisses and telling me to be a good boy. I gave her some extra enthusiastic wet face mushes to let her know I'd miss her. They were up and going a lot earlier than normal and when I didn't get breakfast before they left I figured dad would be back soon or I'd have a lunch date with gramma. They were out the door and gone.

I had nothing else to do and it was early even for me so I decided to go back to sleep. When I woke up dad still wasn't home and gramma hadn't gotten there. I was pretty hungry but I just relaxed on Blankets Mountain and waited. I kept watching the door but time kept on ticking away and it never opened.

I finally heard a key in the lock and then dad came back inside. He was grumbling something about how horrible Atlanta traffic was and muttering some of those words I'm not supposed to hear. He grabbed Graces leash and took her out. When he came back in he went to the kitchen and I heard him open up one of my cans of food.

I got excited and stood up in anticipation. Dad carried me to my ledge on the cat tree and got ready to feed me. When he got the food piled up like a mountain on my plate I sniffed at it. It didn't smell like my usual food and I didn't like it. I turned my head away to let him know I wasn't going to eat that. He didn't seem to understand at first so I sniffed it again, looked at him, and turned away again.

He figured out what the issue was right away. He got up went back into the kitchen, got me my regular kind of food and tried again. I ate that just fine. Once I was done I heard him call gramma and ask her if she'd like a bunch of cans of food. I knew from the past that if I got food I didn't like they'd see if gramma wanted it and if she didn't they'd take it to a local cat rescue. It sounded like those cans were going to the cat rescue but that made me happy because I knew that it would be appreciated there. I remembered how hard it could be at times for KT to get enough food for Misfits Critter Farm.

We had a fun weekend. Dad and I watched a bunch of scary movies that mum didn't like and we played a lot with feathers. Dad made sure everyone got extra treats when I did. After we finished watching the movies I got a notion and decided it was time for an adventure.

I saw Amelia sleeping on top of the couch cushions where I usually jump up to when I'm playing with my feathers at night. I decided I would go and see if she wanted to play. I climbed down Blankets Mountain and made my way across the couch to the bottom of the cushions below her. I thought that the most fun way to ask her to play would be to jump up and give her a scare. After all we had just finished watching a bunch of scary movies so I thought it would be fun to do the scaring.

I got in my crouching stance, did a little but wiggle and jumped up to her. I landed right on top of the cushion next to her and it sure did surprise her. It surprised her so much that she didn't even hiss. Her eyes snapped open and she bolted. She made one huge jump off the cushion and ran to the top of the cat tree. When she jumped off the cushion she accidentally gave it a push and with me on the edge it started to fall over. The cushion came crashing down and I got thrown off of it.

I flew clear off the couch and bounced on the side of the coffee table before I landed on the floor. Dad picked me up before I even completely registered what had happened. He brushed me off and sat down with me. He looked me over but not the way mum would have. He didn't pull on my legs or anything he just pet me and rubbed my sides. I started singing to let him know I was alright. He put the cushion back, straightened up the couch and told me we wouldn't share that part of our weekend with mum. I agreed with him that there was no need to worry mum over that little event.

The next day I had fun adventuring back and forth across the top cushions of the couch again. Dad kept an eye on me and pulled the coffee table out a little farther away from the couch so if I did a repeat of yesterday at least I wouldn't bump into it. Dad told me to get that top of the cushion climbing out of my system today because mum would be home tomorrow and she got stressed out when I did my daredevil adventures.

I was really excited the next day when mum got home. She didn't even put her suitcases in the bedroom. As soon as she walked in the door she came right over to see me. I got a lot of luvins and kisses before she decided to put her things away. She spent the rest of the day spending lots of time with me. That night we decided that since I'd made so many new friends on Facebook that we'd ask everyone to post a picture of their pet.

I had a great time that night. Mum spent the night showing me picture after picture of everyone's pets. Something I don't think most of my friends realized about my posts was that when I start my posts and say "Hai my furiends" I'm telling all of the pets hi. At the end of my posts when I say "Sleep with angels tonight my friends." I'm wishing all of my people friends to be watched over by the angels while they sleep. I always thought it was important to make sure I talked to all of my friends, both four and two legged.

Just a few days later and I got a big surprise in the middle of the day when the door opened and in walked my gramma with my Grammy from South Carolina right behind her! I had forgotten that she was going to be visiting but was really happy to see her. I stood right up and watched Grace get super excited. Her tail was wagging wildly and she was hopping up and down. Grammy seemed surprised that Grace remembered her so well but all of us had such a good time when she was here last year that we all remembered her.

Gramma helped Grammy get Grace calmed down and all of her bags into her room. I remembered that Grammy had an allergy to cat and she was quick to get the bedroom door closed so Leroy wouldn't try to climb in her bags. Gramma got a bone for Grammy to give Grace and this helped her to calm down a bit.

Leroy and Amelia came in to see what the commotion was. Grammy remembered where mum kept the treats in her desk drawer and she went over and out a bag of Temptations. She gave all of us our treats and even got Grace one of her treats. She came over to sit down with me and gramma reminded her about checking the couch so she wouldn't sit in anything (my business) she didn't want to. I got luvins while they talked and after a few minutes gramma went home.

Grammy got her laptop out and sat down next to Blankets Mountain so she could be near me. She hung out with me and played some games on her computer while she waited for dad to get home. Dad and gramma talked for a while. When mum got home she started getting my dinner ready. I ate quickly because I wanted to go spend more time with Grammy.

When mum set me down to do my business I tried to hurry to get that done too. But when I tried to get back to Blankets Mountain I accidentally dragged my entire chest and belly through my business. Mum and Grammy saw it right away but mum couldn't get to me in time. She yelled for dad to grab a towel and get the sink ready because I was getting a bath.

Dad didn't question a thing; he just sprang into action and by the time mum got me to the sink he already had the temperature of the water right and the entire thing ready to go. Grammy was holding her nose at the smell I'd made and when dad saw it he went over and got the mess cleaned up. He got done before mum was finished giving me my bath so he helped her get things finished up.

I was so frustrated. Grammy hadn't even been there an entire day and mum was giving me a bath right in front of her! Mum could have at least taken me to another sink where I wasn't on such public display. Mum asked Grammy to turn on the electric blanket while she finished up my bath. Mum told Grammy I hadn't made a mess that bad in a long time. She worked on drying me with the towel until the blanket started to warm up. Then she set me down on it.

I spent the next hour trying to get my fur dried up and looking right again. Everyone sat around the couch and chatted while they watched a movie. When I got dry enough, I decided that I couldn't let something like a sink bath keep me from getting my feather play time in. Grammy liked to watch me play. I made her laugh when I jumped up high to catch those feathers. By the end of the night we'd all forgotten about the bath and had enjoyed a fun night.

The next day we all enjoyed a nice breakfast. I made sure to take my time and be extra careful after doing my business so I wouldn't have to get another embarrassing sink bath in front of Grammy. I got more treats and belly rubs before lunch than I normally did all day long. After lunch, everyone went out. Dad said they were going to see a movie and if you see a movie in the day time it's called a matinee. I thought that it was odd that they had a different word for the seeing the same movie but just during the day. I just chalked it up to something else new that I got to learn about humans.

When they got home they were in a good mood. Grammy said she had really enjoyed the movie and wanted to watch some other movies on TV next. I liked the sound of that because that meant a much earlier than normal couch time. That would mean extra feathers time! I was right, mum fed me dinner and then everyone sat down to watch movies. I got hours of feathers time and even a bonus round of treats right before everyone went to bed.

The next day was just as fun. They went out for lunch and to do some shopping and I took advantage of it to get caught up on my naps. When they came back, Grammy brought me a couple new feather toys. I knew that meant I'd get a great night of playing again. I was sad the next morning when Grammy said she had to go back home. I made sure she got some extra loud purrs and some super hard wet face mushes.

Things got back to our normal routine after Grammy left. I was pretty comfortable with my normal routine. I actually really enjoyed it! Of course there were lots of interruptions to those normal days and that sure did keep things interesting. A few days after Grammy left, mum came home and she was on the phone with gramma. Once mum hung up with gramma she told dad to get ready to help because gramma was coming over and bringing one of her cats, Meghan, with her. Her nails had gone too long since they had been trimmed and gramma and gramma-great couldn't do it without help.

I wondered why they needed help giving Meghan a nail trim. Mum and dad usually didn't have any problems with any of us. Apparently, Meghan really hated nail trims and would bite at gramma when she tried to clip them. Mum used to be a vet technician for about 10 years in another life, so she knew some secrets of the trade. Grace got super stressed when she got her nails trimmed. They would roll her over on her back and put her head on dads lap. He'd rub her ears and tell her it was okay while mum got the trimming done. Amelia didn't like it either and sometimes dad would have to hold her still. Neither I nor Leroy gave mum any issues. We just sat there and waited for her to get it over with. Every now and then I would give her a meow in protest but as long as it wasn't a sink bath I wasn't much for complaining.

Dad unlocked the door so gramma could just walk in and mum got some towels and blankets to place them on the floor in the living room. Grace was curious about what was going on and laid down on the blankets. When gramma came in, dad moved Grace off the blankets. Gramma had Meghan in a carrier and she set her down in the middle of the living room. She asked mum how they were going to do this and mum took charge.

Gramma opened up the carrier and pulled Meghan out. Meghan took one look at Grace, flattened her ears on her head and gave her a savage hiss. Dad told Grace to go lay down and mum started wrapping Meghan up in a towel. I knew from all of the sink baths I have received, that mum was a black belt in towel wrapping. She had Meghan wrapped up tight before she even realized what was going on. Mum handed her back to gramma and dad handed over the nail trimmers.

Mum started working to getting one of Meghan's front feet freed from the towel. Once it was out, she took a look at it and said a word I'm not supposed to hear. I was watching from Blankets Mountain and had a great view. When mum pressed on the center of her paw I watched her nails pop out. They were super long and curling back towards her foot pad but not touching it.

That was when Meghan let out the most insidious and angry growl I'd ever heard. She hissed and spit and started thrashing around in the towel. I thought gramma was going to lose her grip for a minute, but mum told her to hold on tight and dad knelt down next to them just in case he needed to scruff Meghan on the back of the neck. Mum started trying to get the clippers onto the nails and each time she got close Meghan would howl and squirm.

Leroy and Amelia came running into the living room to see what was going on. Leroy jumped up next to me to make sure I was okay and Amelia climbed up to the top of the cat tree to watch from there. Mum finally got one of the nails clipped and Meghan screamed so loud she scared Leroy. His eyes went huge and he ran as fast as he could into the bedroom. Amelia jumped down from the cat tree onto the couch and sat next to me on Blankets Mountain while she continued to watch. Grace started whining and tried to nose in and sniff Meghan, but dad told her to go lay down again, so she backed up a few steps and sat.

Mum kept working at those nails and each time she got one trimmed Meghan went into an angry frenzy. I didn't understand why she was having such a fit about the nail trim. Mum was really good at it and knew what she was doing. She wasn't even coming close to her quicks but Meghan just got more worked up the longer it went on.

She finally got both of Meghan's front feet done and gramma looked like she was getting tired of wrestling with the towels. When they tried to start to get the back feet out Meghan began fighting harder than she had yet. Dad had to move in and scruff her behind her neck. He gently lifted her up and gramma held her tight. Mum started working on the back feet and Meghan made one last chance to get away. Dad just about got bit and had to move quick to get a better grip. Grace kept whining but stayed where she was. Mum worked as quickly as she could and managed to get the job done. She helped gramma get Meghan angled and let her run back into her carrier. Once she was in it she turned around and hissed at everyone. She then turned to the back of the carrier, sat there and sulked.

I wasn't even sure what to think. Meghan never gave me the impression she could be so ugly while I spent those two days over at grammas. She even sat in grammas lap and got her luvins. I guess she really just didn't like to have her nails trimmed. Mum, dad and gramma sure were glad it was over with and gramma gave mum a big hug before she took Meghan home.

Grace settled down and went to take a nap next to the glass door. Amelia must have gotten confused with all of the noise Meghan had made because she curled up next to me on Blankets Mountain and took a nap with me. We had a nice nap, but when she started to wake up her tail started flipping around and she kept smacking me in the face with it. I eventually got tired of it and gave her a bite on her butt. She got surprised, hissed at me and ran off to the bedroom.

Later that week I started getting cards and packages in the mail again. Mum sat down with me and opened up the cards. She read them to me and they were from another holiday I was getting to learn about called Easter. Mum explained what Easter was and how some people celebrated it and some people didn't. I had friends from all over the world so not everyone did and mum said that was okay.

She told me that just like I was different there were a lot of differences between people in different cultures.

She explained to me that all of those differences made the world a more interesting place. She told me if we were all the same things would get boring quickly. She also explained that sometimes those differences kept people from getting along and being friends. She said that was one of the things that made me and my Facebook page special. She said that people could listen to my stories, and despite having some differences that would normally keep them from ever speaking, they could share something that was universal; which was love.

Chapter Eight – The Garbage Bag Monster

Neuro Dan - Feather Dan
April 6, 2016 ·

Hai my furiends. Mum pulled out a new great big FEATHER that one of my friends sent me. Iz been chomping on it and talking to it and jumping after it and having a great time. I think Amelia is going to come help me play with it she's been watching for a minute now. I hope you are all having a great week. Sleep with the angels tonight my friends. I luvs you.

Dad was always trying to keep me entertained and let me try new things. Letting me try different kinds of foods was one of the ways he did that. Every now and then I would get in a picky mood and not feel like eating. When that happened mum and dad would go to the pantry where they kept all my canned food and find something different. Sometimes it would work and I'd get a sniff of something that got my interest, but more often than not, I didn't care for the new stuff. As a result I wound up with a shelf full of food that mum knew I didn't like and wouldn't eat.

She got her own notion one day and decided that if I wasn't going to eat it there was no reason to keep it in the house. There was enough of it that it was taking up quite a bit of space. Since we are always trying to find ways to help others she decided that she would bag it all up and take it to the local cat shelter where she knew it would be greatly appreciated.

She had several bags of food by the time she was done gathering it up. She must have been getting in that spring cleaning mode too because she took a stack of old newspapers that dad hadn't gotten around to recycling yet. It took her two trips to get everything up to her car. She gave me a kiss on the head and told me she was off to the shelter but she'd be back soon.

I decided to take a nap while she was gone so I'd be rested up in case she wanted to play with feathers when she got back. When she did get back I figured out I was right about her getting the spring cleaning bug because she spent a few hours cleaning everywhere. Once she decided she was done she plopped down on the couch next to me and gave me luvins for a while.

She realized it was pretty close to my dinner time so she decided to go ahead and feed me. She went into the kitchen. I heard her moving stuff around in the pantry then she said one of those words I'm not supposed to hear. She came back out and told me she accidentally gave all of my food to the shelter. I gave her my best stern look to let her know I still expected my dinner. She grabbed her car keys and said she'd be back.

She wasn't gone too long and she came home with a bunch of my favorite canned foods. I ate all of my dinner and even got some treats later that night. Mum told dad what she'd done and dad got a good laugh out of it. We played with my feathers and had a fun night.

The next day I got a notion. I had been thinking about how much fun I had climbing the cat tree when it had been pulled up next to Blankets Mountain. I'd been studying it and decided I wanted to see if I could get up it again. Mum and dad had gone to the grocery store so I decided I'd give it a try.

I got down off Blankets Mountain and made my way over to the cat tree. I put my front feet up on the ledge I eat on, hopped and clawed my way up it. I rested there for a bit while I thought about my best move to get to the ledge above me. I tried a couple of different maneuvers but didn't have any luck. I studied it some more and tried again.

I tried to climb the post. I clung onto it with my claws and tried to go paw over paw. I made it up about a foot and that's when the front door opened. I must have been trying longer than I thought because mum and dad were already home from shopping. Mum saw me right away, dropped her bags and rushed over to me. She picked me up and told me not to climb up like that.

Dad laughed and got the groceries put up while mum set me back on Blankets Mountain and gave me some luvins. When dad was done he came over to see me. He picked me up and set me all the way up on top of the cat tree. He didn't even need to get a chair he just reached up and set me there. Mum gave him a funny look and told him not to encourage me. Dad said I was fine and stood by me for a while and let me look around. I had a great time too. Sometimes you just want to see things from a different perspective.

The next day we got a gramma visit! It was such a nice day outside that her and mum decided to go sit on the porch and talk. Mum thought that I would probably enjoy sitting outside with them so she picked me up, carried me out and set me in her lap. We stayed out there for a long time. There were lots of birds flying around. They were singing and chirping. They flew from tree to tree and hopped around on the ground. I got so excited that mum thought my whiskers were going to be stuck in flex mode all night.

Dad checked the mail on his way home and when he walked in the door he told mum I had another package. Mum took it and opened it up. It was another long tube and knew that those packages usually had feathers in them. This one did too. It had a great big beautiful peacock feather. Dad could tell I was super excited and he came and played with me early that night. I played extra hard with my new peacock feather. Amelia even got interested and she watched for quite a while. She even jumped up and played with me and she didn't even hiss.

The next night mum was helping me post my story on Facebook and she told me my page had over 5000 friends on it now. I sure was surprised. I still couldn't believe how much people liked to hear me tell my stories. That made me feel good inside and I smiled a lot that night. Getting so happy also caused me to get a little excited and that started to give me a notion. I was planning out an adventure for the weekend but wasn't sure exactly what I wanted to do yet.

I thought about it all night and decided that it had been too long since I'd been on a floor adventure and tried to scare mum and dad. I waited until Leroy and Amelia finished their last patrol of the night and just before the sun came up. I climbed down off Blankets Mountain and looked around for a fun spot to hide. I walked over to the cat tree and hid behind it for a while. I didn't think mum and dad would think to look for me there first but there wasn't really anything to get good and hidden behind.

I thought it over and decided I would go and get behind mums desk. I knew that would be one of the first places she looked but if I got behind it she wouldn't be able to see me just by looking. When she went to get a closer look I'd be able to jump out and surprise her. I started making my way over to the desk. It took me about twenty minutes but I finally got there. Just as I was starting to walk behind it mum came out of the bedroom and saw me. She told me I was being a rascal and giggled at me. I snuck behind the desk anyway because I thought maybe I could still surprise dad.

Dad came out just a few minutes later. He looked at Blankets Mountain and when he didn't see me he stopped and started glancing around. I snuck my head out from behind the desk to see what he was doing but I had bad timing and he saw me just as I poked my head out. I guess I wasn't going to be doing any sneaky surprises but they both got a good chuckle out of my antics so at least I got them to smile before they even had their coffee.

That night I figured since I didn't manage to scare either mum or dad that I would try to get them to get the special treats from England out. I was always in the mood for treats but I had a craving for one of those beef sticks. I kept giving mum the eyes and I made sure I ate a good dinner so she would be proud of me.

I played feathers but kept stopping. I would give mum and dad the eyes and then turn and stare at mum's desk. Specifically I would stare at the top right drawer. I knew that's where they were and I always kept a close eye on that drawer so nothing would happen to them. I never knew when Amelia would get extra hungry when the food bowl ran low and try to break into the treats.

Mum got the message but told me I only had a few of those left and she was saving them for a special occasion. I didn't think I needed a special occasion, especially not if I was having a craving. During my Facebook post that night I asked all of my friends to help me convince her to let me have a special treat. By the time mum got done reading all of the comments the next day she couldn't help but to give in. She told me I was a stinker and hundreds of people were helping me beg for my treat. I had to wait for that night but I got my treat!

Between getting my treat and playing extra hard with my feathers and dad I got super tired. I actually fell asleep while I was reaching for a feather. Remember I mentioned that my eyes don't close all the way when I sleep? Well they stayed open pretty wide that time. Mum didn't really think I was asleep and when she wasn't sure she would wiggle a feather in front of me. She knows I can't resist a feather so if I'm just relaxing I would swipe for the feather but if I was actually asleep I wouldn't move. I was sound asleep that time and didn't even see her wiggle the feathers. She took a picture and the next day when she shared it with me; I had to agree that I looked pretty goofy.

The next day was Saturday and I was looking forward to my extra play time with dad. He usually spends the day at home cleaning the house, doing laundry and of course playing with me all day long in between chores. That day he got up early for a Saturday, got his coffee and then fed me my breakfast. When I was done and back on Blankets Mountain he gathered up some papers from his desk gave me a kiss on the head and left out the front door.

I thought maybe he was just out getting his errands done early but I waited and waited and he still didn't come home. I napped for a while to pass the time and when I woke up it was almost time for my dinner. I looked around to see if he came in and I just didn't wake up but there was still no one home. I just couldn't imagine why he would have to be gone so long on a day off. I couldn't see what could possibly be more important than getting in some extra feathers time. He wasn't even wearing his work clothes so I knew he hadn't gone to work.

A little more time passed and I knew, by how hungry I was that it was very close to my dinner time. When he finally came home he had even more papers with him and looked grumpy. He put the papers on the kitchen table and quickly got Grace hooked up to her leash and took her out. When he came back he put his papers in some kind of a file and took them to the closet.

He came over and gave me luvins. He told me he had to deal with Uncle Sam and it took longer than he thought it would. I didn't remember him or mum ever talking about any Uncle Sam. I wasn't sure who this Uncle was but I was going to tell dad that unless Uncle Sam played with feathers that he could just wait until after feathers time is done next time he needs something.

After dad got me dinner and I was back up on Blankets Mountain he went into the kitchen to take care of some chores. He washed the dishes and pulled out the full trash bag. Amelia happened to be wandering over to the food bowl when he was getting ready to put the new trash bag in the can. He gave the trash bag one great big shake to get it to open up. He didn't see Amelia and it made a loud scary pop right above her and bumped her on her back.

Amelia absolutely freaked out! She jumped in the air with her legs scrambling. When she hit the ground she hit the ground running. She ran into the kitchen but dad hadn't seen her yet and while she was trying to find an escape route dad gave the bag another shake. It made a loud popping sound again and Amelia got even more scared. She jumped up on the kitchen table, raced across it and leaped all the way onto the back of the couch.

Dad started to give the bag one more shake but he saw Amelia in a panic and stopped. She ran down the end of the couch, dove on mum's desk and wiped out. Her feet were pedaling fast but with all the commotion Grace jumped up and barked at her. Amelia didn't slow down one bit. She jumped down to the floor and was headed for the bedroom but Grace was running at her. She turned and jumped back up onto the couch. She ran as fast as she could across the top of the couch and sprinted right at me! I was already standing up watching the fun and Amelia crashed right into me and knocked me down!

I almost fell off Blankets Mountain but I managed to dig in my claws and hold on. I chattered at her to let her know I didn't appreciate that she tried to throw me to the garbage bag monster. Amelia jumped up to the cat tree and immediately dropped to the floor. Grace spun around and was right behind her. Amelia ran as fast as she could toward the front of the house and the guest bedroom. Grace ran into the bedroom behind her and came back out a couple of seconds later.

Dad got a good laugh out of that and he shook out the trash bag one last time before he got it in the can. He came over to Blankets Mountain and sat with me for a little bit. We had fun playing with some feathers and he showed me a couple of places where he'd hidden some feathers that I hadn't found yet. Mum got a good chuckle out of Amelia's antics that night while we were enjoying couch time. It took Amelia until almost bed time before she came back out. At least she was lucky and Grace had forgotten about the incident and didn't try to give her a pit maneuver.

Mum told me that dad was going to get another three day weekend again but it might not be as fun as the last few. She said he had a dentist appointment in the morning. I'd never been to the dentist but mum told me that I might need to be extra sweet to dad because the he was going to be getting a lot done to his teeth. I sure was hoping he was going to be okay. If his teeth hurt he wouldn't be able to chomp on feathers or eat treats and I couldn't imagine he could have a very good weekend without being able to do that.

The next day when he came back from the dentist he looked absolutely miserable. His cheeks were puffy and it looked like he'd been bleeding. He looked exhausted and he must have been because he didn't even take Grace out or say hi to me he just went and sat down at his desk and didn't do anything.

Mum got home early that day. She and dad talked and dad sounded funny. Mum took Grace out and sat with me while they chatted. Mum did most of the talking and dad did quite a bit of grunting or nodding and shaking his head. They sat down on the couch pretty early that day and I noticed dad didn't even eat his dinner. I hoped he was okay because mum always makes a big deal out of things if I miss a meal or don't eat well.

They watched T.V. for a while and a show about a guy named Jackson Galaxy called "My Cat from H. E. double hockey sticks came on. Mum says I'm not allowed to use those bad words so I have to improvise when I need to. That guy goes to people's houses who have kitties that have some pretty bad behavior issues and he helps their humans figure things out and help them get better. I thought that sounded like a wonderful show and was definitely something I was interested in watching.

At first I enjoyed it but then some cats started making really angry noises. I wasn't expecting that and it made me jump up and get ready for a confrontation. Leroy came trotting out from the bedroom and Amelia popped her head up from the top of the cat tree. Grace didn't seem to mind. She was curled up in the middle of the living room. Her ears twitched but other than that she didn't move. The noises got louder and scarier. Leroy hopped up next to me on Blankets Mountain to make sure I was okay. I sure did like the way he always came to check on me when he thought something was wrong.

He sat with me for a little while and mum said she thought it was really sweet. She tried to tell us it was just the T.V. but the sounds were real and it still got us defensive. I wanted to tell those angry kitties that life is too short to make scary noises. I've always found that you get a whole lot more treats and feathers by giving sweet eyes and good purrs than by being mad.

Chapter Nine – The Giant Dinosaur Goose

Neuro Dan - Feather Dan

May 12, 2016 ·
Hi everyone, mum here. I go through day to day troubles and at times I think it is more than I can bear. Then I look at this lil one and know I am wrong. Every day, he struggles to move, but somehow does it without complaint. He is never in a bad mood. He is always eager to greet us with smiles and an obvious eagerness. He never accepts evil in his life and he loves without boundaries. We humans have so much to learn from those who live with such challenges.

The next morning I was sitting on my ledge getting my breakfast. I was hungry and eating good which always made mum happy. I was about half way through my meal when a terrible racket and commotion happened right outside the glass door. It was a loud vibrating and whining sound that kept revving over and over again. It scared me good and I hopped up, turned around and glared at whatever was on the other side of the glass door.

Grace had been sitting on the floor next to mum, waiting to see if I'd drop her any food and she got scared too. She barked and jumped up so quickly she bumped her head on the bottom of my ledge. She barked over and over again and almost ran mum over as she charged at the glass door. Leroy and Amelia both ran off into the bedroom so fast I barely saw their tails disappear around the corner.

Grace was really letting the landscaper have it. She was right up to the glass door, crouched and barking savagely at them. I don't know if they could hear her or not but mum sure could and she was yelling at her to stop it and be quiet. I could have told mum she was wasting her breath because there was no way Grace was going to be calm with all of that commotion right there. They were just lucky she couldn't get outside because as worked up as she was, I was pretty certain they'd all be getting the pit maneuver.

Mum told me it was okay, that it was just the landscapers, but I was having none of it. I've heard them come through the yard before but I usually hear them coming from a long ways away so I'm ready for them when they get close. This time they just started everything up right outside our apartment. There were a lot of people with different machines. Some of them had things they were riding and others had things they were holding but all of them were making really loud and frightful noises.

One of them ran something right up along the edge of the porch and made grass and dirt fly all over. That was enough for me;

I was heading for higher ground! I looked at Blanket's Mountain and thought about making a jump for it. I glanced behind me and thought about climbing to the top of the cat tree. I decided on jumping up to Blankets Mountain.

I crouched and was about to make a jump for it when mum set my food down and scooped me up. She was fussing at the landscapers but I was pretty sure they were making too much noise to be able to hear her. She set me down on Blankets Mountain and sat with me until they were finally far enough away that we couldn't hear them anymore. Grace finally stopped barking, but she stayed in front of the glass door and made an occasional growl just to make sure they didn't come back.

Mum picked me up again and set me back on my ledge. She got my plate of food, piled it back up into the shape of a mountain and tried to get me to eat again. I wanted nothing to do with food and was still pretty jumpy from having been scared; so I got up and turned right back around. I continued to glare at the glass door. Mum grumbled again at the landscapers and set my food back down. She got me back up on Blankets Mountain and told me I needed to make sure I ate a good dinner that night. She set the rest of my food down for Leroy and Amelia. She gave me a kiss on the head, grabbed her keys and hurried off to work. Gramma came by later that day to try to get me to eat again. But I was still too perturbed to eat and turned around to face away from her too.

I spent the rest of the day practicing making scary faces. I didn't know who those landscapers thought they were, but if they decided to start all of their machines right in front of our apartment again, I was going to have to do something to scare them off. If I could work on scary faces and get it down perfect, I'd march up to the glass door with Grace and tell them to beat it.

I made sure to show mum and dad my scary faces that night. I wanted them to help me choose which one to use if those landscapers came back again. Dad took a bunch of pictures of me doing my scary faces and mum showed me which ones she thought were the most savage. She shared my scariest face with my Facebook friends that night and told them about the rude landscapers. My friends agreed that I could make a mean, savage face and it would surely get the point across that they needed to leave.

The next night when dad came home, he said a note had been left on our front door. He told mum that there workers were going to be pressure washing the outside steps and patio the next day. Mum sat down with me and told me that meant there were going to be more scary noises. Mum and dad wouldn't be home and without knowing what time the pressure washers would be there, they couldn't get gramma to come and sit with me. She told me that meant I'd have to be brave. Well I'd been practicing my scary face so if they didn't get it done fast, I was going to let them have it.

As it turned out they did get the pressure washing done really fast. Dad pulled all of the outside patio furniture inside so it wouldn't be in the way. Leroy and Amelia were fascinated with the outside furniture suddenly being inside. They spent the morning climbing all over it. When the pressure washers got there they were lounging and relaxing.

As soon as the first water blast hit the patio chaos ensued. They both scrambled to their feet, eyes wide and in a panic, trying to figure out which way to run. Grace had been asleep in the middle of the living room and she jumped to her feet with a muffled woof. The woofs turned into rapid-fire barks and she lunged towards the glass door. Leroy and Amelia started their panicked escape at the same time and all three of them got tangled together. Amelia wound up running towards the guest bedroom and Leroy zipped around the corner into mum and dads bedroom.

I stood up and looked intently at the porch. I was getting ready to make my scary face to get them to leave but they were done with the porch before I had a chance. I could hear them talk as they walked over towards the front door and the stairs. The pressure washers started getting the siding by the back bedroom. Grace turned her attention from the glass door and started her charge towards the front door. Poor Amelia shot out of the guest bedroom as fast as she could and ran right into Grace again. Grace ignored her and let her run away. She ran past me and back towards where Leroy had gone.

It didn't take them long at all to do whatever it was they were doing. Grace finally got calmed down but stayed extra vigilant and gave out random warning barks for the rest of the day. When dad got home he put the outside furniture back on the patio. Grace went out with him and sniffed around to make sure nothing was hiding out there that would make any more noises. That seemed to do the trick to convince her nothing was hiding outside and she finally quit doing those random barks.

I guess the yard looked good and the stairs were cleaned enough because things got quiet and went back to normal for the next few days. Mum told me that in about a month I was going to have a birthday and I'd be turning two years old. Those doctors told me I would be lucky to live to be two years old and I was feeling fantastic. Sure I had my struggles because of my special needs, but I was going strong and having the time of my life!

Mum told me that my super positive attitude and perseverance was still an inspiration to many people. I also thought that all of the love I got from my Facebook friends was helping me too. Every time I had a bad day or it looked like my disease was progressing mum would ask my friends for prayers and positive thoughts. It never took long after that before I bounced right back to feeling great again. Mum told me she was going to try to do something special to surprise me with on my birthday. I was curious what she was thinking but I knew she could keep a surprise a secret for a long time. I decided to try to get some extra treats since she was making me wait.

I got a different kind of surprise that weekend. Dad was home and doing his chores. He had a couple of loads of laundry going, had already gotten the vacuum monster out of the way and had just sat down at his desk to rest when an incredibly strange sound erupted from the back of the kitchen near the laundry room. It sounded like the roar of some kind of a giant dinosaur goose!

I jumped up right away and looked in that direction. Grace sprung to her feet and barked as she charged into the kitchen. Dad got startled too and said a word I should have covered my ears for. He got up and followed behind Grace into the kitchen. Amelia had been napping on mum's desk chair and I think she was still half asleep as she scrambled away into the bedroom.

Just as Grace rounded the corner into the kitchen the monster stopped screaming. It only stopped for a second though. I guess it was taking another breath because it did that same roar again right away. Grace got even more excited and was barking faster and louder than ever.

I stepped up onto the back of the couch and cautiously walked towards the wall to try to get a look into the kitchen. I had to see what a giant dinosaur goose looked like! I bet it had some impressive feathers. Dad told Grace to get out of the way and a second later the noise stopped. Grace was still barking but dad told her to shush and she finally did. She followed him back to his desk. Dad gave her a new chew bone to take her mind off of the invasion of the giant dinosaur goose.

I made myself comfortable on the cushion up against the wall where dad usually sat. I had a decent view of the kitchen and could keep an eye on things from there. I didn't see anything at the moment but I wasn't going to turn my back on it anytime soon. Leroy wandered out from the bedroom. He must have been sound asleep because he was moving slow and blinking his eyes. He looked at me and I told him that he should go patrol the kitchen because a giant dinosaur goose had been roaring and it took Grace and dad both to get it to stop.

I didn't know if it went away or just hid. I had no idea how something like that could get in the house without one of us seeing it. It couldn't have snuck in at night or I'm sure that Leroy or Amelia would have seen it on one of their patrols. It was very unlikely anything like that could get past Grace during the day.

Dad finally noticed me sitting at the other end of the couch and staring into the kitchen. He came over and sat with me for a little while. He told me that the noise was nothing to be afraid of that he just bumped the end of cycle alarm on the drier and it had gone off. It was usually kept off and that's why it normally didn't make any noises at all. I had no idea what he was talking about but I did have a pretty good idea of what a giant dinosaur goose would sound like and I was pretty certain that's exactly what it was. I planned on waiting until after everyone went to bed so I could go investigate it for myself.

Leroy went into the kitchen, came out looked around then hopped up on the table where his food bowl was and started eating. Dad went back to his desk and worked on his computer. Grace curled up by his feet and chewed on her bone. Amelia didn't come back out for a couple of hours and when she did she was jumpy. She stayed jumpy for the rest of the night. It had been one heck of a week with the crazy noises around here and I figured it would be a good idea to keep on practicing my scary faces.

While I kept an eye on the kitchen, dad told me that tomorrow was Mother's Day. I knew this was one of those important traditions that I liked so well. Dad was pretty good at helping me remember them. He told me he was going to go out and get some things to surprise mum with. I wondered what he was going to get and where he was going to hide them this time. Mum was sure to get curious and since she hates surprises and dad is so good at surprising her, she would surely be on the hunt when she got back from work.

Dad wasn't gone very long and when he came back, he showed me the card he got for her. He always made sure he got one from him and got another card that was from me, Leroy, Amelia and Grace. He told me I was in charge of guarding the cards. I wasn't sure what he meant, but he lifted up part of Blankets Mountain and hid them between some blankets. He was sneaky! I would have to make sure to keep mum distracted and try not to make them replace too many blankets on the couch that night.

He also had some flowers. He took some into the guest bedroom to one of his sneaky hiding spots she hadn't found yet and put the others on the living room table. He told me those were for gramma and gramma-great. He also had a card for them and said that he would leave that out for mum to fill out. I could already tell everyone was going to be in a good mood tomorrow. I wondered if I'd get to see gramma and gramma-great or if mum and dad would be going over to their place.

I was still keeping my attention on the kitchen. I wasn't going to let that sneaky giant dinosaur goose get past me. I had to do double duty during feathers time that night. Between keeping mum distracted from finding her cards and watching out for the giant dinosaur goose I didn't get quite as much feather pouncing as I normally would have. That was okay though because I was just waiting on mum and dad to go to bed so I could go investigate.

After they went to bed I didn't waste any time. I climbed down Blankets Mountain. Then I slowly backed up to the edge of the couch and lower myself down. I decided to stay close to the couch so I would blend in, and if either mum or dad walked across the hall to go to the bathroom they wouldn't spot me. I followed the couch until I could see into the dining room area and made my way over there.

I stopped next to the trash can and rested for a minute. This was a big adventure for me. First of all I didn't really like the kitchen. That's where I always got my sink baths. There was also nothing interesting in there and there was no way out except the way you go in. I guess it didn't bother Amelia and Leroy because they just jumped up on the counter and crossed into the living room that way whenever they wanted to.

I took another couple of steps forward and peaked around the counter into the kitchen. I didn't see anything unusual at all. The pantry closet at the end of the kitchen was closed like usual. The washer and drier were at the end by the closet on the right. The sliding doors that hid them were closed so I couldn't tell if anything was there or not. I decided I needed to get a better look. I made my way into the kitchen.

I looked in every nook and cranny I could to see if maybe the giant dinosaur goose had dropped any feathers. I didn't see anything so I kept on going until I was right next to the sliding doors that hid the washer and drier. I listened intently but there were no noises at all. Nothing smelled out of place either. I knew that the feathers my friends sent me all had different scents depending on what type of feathers they were. I thought maybe I'd find some evidence in an odd smell but I didn't.

I decided to be brave and see if I could push open one of the sliding doors. I got to the end of the one by the closet and started working it with my paws. I got it to swing a little and it rattled some as it bounced around. I kept on working at it and it slid open just a bit. I stopped and waited to make sure nothing was going to jump out at me. I listened again but still didn't hear anything so I went back to working on getting the door to slide open a little more.

I must have been making more noise than I thought because Leroy hopped up on the kitchen counter from the living room. He walked over to the stove and was looking down at me wanting to know what I was doing. I told him I was looking for what had made that noise earlier. I told him I was sure that it was a giant dinosaur goose and that it was probably hiding in here.

Leroy dropped down off the stove onto the floor and came over to me. He gave me a couple of kisses on top of my head then walked up to the sliding door where I had gotten it to open a little. He shoved his head into the door and gave it a good hard push. He got it to open and kept pushing until the entire drier was exposed. Then jumped up on top of it and looked around.

I looked around too. Neither of us saw anything at all that resembled a giant dinosaur goose. I did discover where mum hid all of my food though. There was a wire shelf way above the drier and I saw all of my favorite foods stacked up almost as high as the ceiling. Well if I couldn't find the beast, at least I knew I had enough food to last me a good long time.

Leroy walked over onto the washing machine and continued to investigate for me. He looked around the corner of the door and shook his head no. There just wasn't anything to find. He came back over and dropped down beside me. I thought about it for a minute and decided maybe it slept at night and was hidden away somewhere. I decided to give it one more shot tomorrow and investigate it during the daytime.

Leroy then trotted off to conduct one of his odd nightly patrols and I started to make my way back to the living room. I wasn't used to walking around that much and I sure was getting tired. I kind of hoped that either mum or dad would get up for a drink, spot me out of place and give me a lift back to Blankets Mountain. That didn't happen though and by the time I got back to the end of the couch near the cat tree, I decided I would just climb up to my ledge and spend the rest of the night there. It would be fun to see mum and dads expression when they found me there anyway. Since my investigation was on hold until tomorrow anyway, I decided to sleep the rest of the night so I would be energized for whatever was next.

Chapter Ten – Birthday Celebration

Neuro Dan - Feather Dan May 25, 2016 ·

Yay! I got mail today. I got birthday cards and a birthday package and there were turkey FEATHERS in it! Mum said I could have one tonight but the other one has to wait until my birthday. So I chomps my new FEATHER with a big smile. I just luvs to chomps the FEATHERS. Sleep with the angels tonight my friends. I luvs you all.

Dad must have been extra tired from banishing that giant dinosaur goose because the next morning mum got up before he did. On special tradition days like Mother's Day he always manages to get up first or sneak out in the middle of the night to put flowers and cards on mum's desk but he slept right through the night this time. Mum came out and immediately noticed that I wasn't on Blankets Mountain.

She looked around for me. Since I wasn't trying to hide, she saw me right away. I stood up and gave her a big smile. She scooped me up and carried me over to my bathroom spot so I could do my business. She disappeared into the kitchen and started making her coffee. When she came out she helped get me back on Blankets Mountain; then went to her desk. She didn't seem to notice that she didn't have flowers or a card on her desk but I didn't think she could have forgotten because their presents for gramma and gramma-great were still on the living room table.

Mum enjoyed her coffee and looked at her computer for about a half hour before dad got up. Grace was right on his heals so he grabbed her leash and out they went. He must have been sleepy still because when mum told him good morning he just grunted. He came back in after a bit and went and got his own cup of coffee. While it was brewing he snuck into the guest bedroom and brought out mums flowers.

He quickly pulled the cards out from Blankets Mountain, snuck up on mum and gave them to her with a hug. Mum made happy noises and told him thank you. She opened the cards and came and gave me a hug and told me thank you too. She sat with me for a minute and told dad about where she'd found me while he got his coffee. He told her I'd been acting odd since that driers alarm went off yesterday. He gave me scratches on the head as he went to sit down at his desk.

Well of course I was acting odd; after all it's not every day you hear a giant dinosaur goose yelling in your kitchen. I couldn't figure out why he and Grace weren't acting odd since they had gone in there to subdue it. I'd been here over a year now and never heard that noise, so I wasn't taking any chances at all.

I watched them chat and get ready to start the day. Dad got me my breakfast and sat down at my ledge to feed me. When finished, he helped me get back to Blankets Mountain. It was at this point that the front door opened. Grace let out a bark and raced to the door. That is when gramma and gramma-great walked through the door! Grace's tail started wagging back and forth and she kept hopping up on her hind legs. Gramma greeted her and then pushed her back enough so they could get inside.

Gramma-great came straight over to Blankets Mountain. Dad was right there and he gave her a big hug. Grace wandered straight over to gramma and dad He got her to leave gramma alone. He then gave gramma a big hug too. Gramma-great stopped for a few minutes to see me. She brought her own treats with her and she started giving me some right away. Leroy and Amelia always could sense when treats were being given because merely seconds passed before they came running too. Once everyone got some treats and some petting gramma and gramma-great came and sat down on the couch.

They talked for a while and mum gave them their flowers and cards. They liked them very much. Dad had even snuck one in there from me, Leroy, Amelia and Grace and they thought that was extra sweet. Dad did a good job because that got us a second round of treats! After a little while they all got up and left together. I figured they were going to go out to eat since that seemed to be a regular tradition for them. I wondered if I would get any snacks from leftovers when they got back.

Once they were gone, I took a little nap. I had a full stomach from just having eaten breakfast and two rounds of treats. When I woke up I decided I needed to go finish my investigation and see if that giant dinosaur goose was hanging out in the kitchen again. Leroy must have known what I was going to do because he was sitting up on the kitchen counter, watching me make my way back into the kitchen. He dropped down and followed me over to the drier where he helped me look around again.

There was still no sign of anything suspicious. I had no idea what the cycle alarm dad had been talking about was but I had to guess that it was the culprit. Maybe that was his name for a giant dinosaur goose. I didn't know but there was nothing left for me to figure out at the moment. If it came back and made that noise again I would charge into action immediately to catch it red handed.

I decided to get back to the living room and see if I could get back up onto Blankets Mountain. My nap must have lasted longer than I thought because I had barely gotten out of the kitchen and into the dining room when mum and dad got home. Mum spotted me right away. She set her bag of leftovers down and walked over to pick me up. She asked me what in the world I was doing way over there, but I wasn't quite sure how to explain that one to her. Leroy was still over there with me and she gave him a funny look. She wanted to know what kind of mischief the two of us had been into. Neither of us gave her a clear answer and she just smiled and shook her head.

Dad took Grace out for a walk and when he came back, he and mum sat down on the couch with me. They spent the rest of the day watching movies. That meant that I got lots of extra play time and treats. Mum and dad were talking about my upcoming birthday and mum said she had an idea. She got on my Facebook page and left my friends a message. She told me that it was part of my birthday surprise and she wasn't going to tell me what she posted until later. Mum always had good ideas and I loved getting surprised so I didn't mind waiting a bit.

A few days later, and for no reason I could figure out, I started feeling funny. I was eating great in the mornings but just didn't have much of an appetite for dinner. As the week went on I started having a little more trouble swallowing my food and my front legs weren't cooperating with me. I would tell my legs to walk like normal, but they were dragging on the ground a bit. I had to take smaller bites when I was eating so I wouldn't choke and cough. It didn't stop me from being happy or wanting to play and chomp on my feathers, but it was slowing me down a bit.

I didn't understand what was happening and mum was getting really worried. She was afraid it was a progression of my neurological disease. She shared what was happening on my Facebook page and I got hundreds of prayers right away. Those prayers and positive thoughts that came from my friends were just amazing. The power they bring is something that is hard for me to understand let alone try to describe.

It took less than twenty four hours for me to start to rebound. As soon as those prayers started coming I started feeling stronger. The next night I ate my dinner like a champ and didn't choke once. My legs started cooperating again and weren't dragging on the ground. My energy levels were off the chart and I think I even played so hard that night that I wore dad out. I guess Amelia could feel how good all of those prayers felt too because she came up on

Blankets Mountain and curled up with me. She had never snuggled with me like that before.

After a few days, mum couldn't even tell that I had been having a neurological decline. She was just as amazed as I was. She had been back on my Facebook page a few times working on whatever my birthday surprise was. I saw her post several pictures of me that I knew were some of her favorites. I saw she asked my friends to vote on them and help her pick out one to use for my surprise. If she had all of my Facebook friends in on it, I knew it was going to be something special. I found myself getting more and more curious about what exactly she had planned.

Dad came home one night and he was laughing when he came in the door. Mum asked him what was going on and he told her it was the mail man. Mum was just as confused as I was until dad came down the hall and we saw he could barely hold all of the mail that he was carrying. He dropped it all over the back of the couch next to Blankets Mountain and told mum I got some mail. Mum couldn't believe the pile that dad had dropped off. I was also really surprised and curious about it.

He came around the couch and pulled out three envelopes. He put those on his desk and told me the rest was all mine. It had only been two days since he checked the mail and he told mum that I had taken up several of the parcel lockers at the mail box. He said that our box was stuffed as full as it could get. The poor mail man must have been having a fit and dad could just imagine the looks he was going to get the next time he saw him.

Mum sat down and started opening envelopes and reading the cards to me. It was a wonderful combination of birthday cards and get well cards. My friends were so sweet that it made my heart warm and made me feel wonderful. I got lots of new feathers toys and even an entire case of my favorite food! There was a package with a new kind of treat in it that I hadn't tried before. Mum let me have some right then and there. It was delicious! It was flaky and tasted like eating a real fish. Mum said those counted as very special treats and there were only a few so they would be mostly for special occasions. I planned on making up a lot of special occasions because those were so good they kept me purring for a long time after I was done.

More mail came in every day for the rest of the month. Dad did a better job of making sure he got to the mail box everyday so the mailman would have room to put other people's packages. Dad didn't want the mailman to have to work so hard at stuffing all the mail in our box. When dad checked the mail on Saturday the mailman was still there. He gave dad a funny look and dad told him that it was my birthday. The mailman shook his head and mumbled something about a cat getting more mail for their birthday than anyone else on his entire route. Dad got a chuckle out of that and so did mum when he told her what the mailman said.

Later that week and a few days before my birthday mum finally told me what my surprise was. She said I was going to be able to team up with another special needs kitty that I was friends with named Clovis and together we are going to "pay it forward". Clovis was going to be eight on the eighth and I was going to be two on the second. We were both told by the vets that we would never live as long as we have, yet here we both were, alive and well!

We were all going to celebrate my birthday by giving back in the same way others have helped us. Our mums have each chosen a small local animal rescue. Clovis chose a rescue named Peanut's Place and my mum chose Floyd Felines and Friends. We were donating our birthdays to those rescues. Anyone who wants to help celebrate and pay it forward could send a donation and we would send them a surprise in the mail. We sent a special thank you post card that had a picture of both me and Clovis on it to anyone who wanted to donate. Mum told me we would continue to do this and celebrate through the entire month of June.

I thought that was absolutely wonderful! One of my favorite things ever was to be able to help other kitties who were in need. There are so many good people and shelters out there who try to help animals that it warms my heart. I remembered being at Misfits Critter Farm with KT before I got lucky enough to get my forever home here. I remembered how hard she worked and how much it cost to keep things going. I was so happy to know that I was going to be able to help a local shelter who was struggling in order to help other cats in need.

I was so excited about how much fun my birthday was going to be that I got a case of the zoomies. I can't do the zoomies like Leroy and Amelia but I do them in my own way. Dad had already played feathers with me for a couple of hours and was getting ready to head to bed, but I was still going strong. I kept on jumping up as high as I could on the couch cushions and I did it over and over again. Mum was watching me and chuckling at how much fun I was having.

Then I got one last good jump in, but I went too high again and went right over the top of the couch and slid down the wall behind it. When mum saw my back legs and tail disappear behind the couch she yelled for dad. He hurried over and pushed the couch out of the way. Mum scooped me up and started doing her systematic check-me-overs to make sure I wasn't hurt. Of course I was fine, but I had learned to just let mum do her inspection so she would feel better. Dad said I was doing those superman jumps a little too often. He went to a closet and got out a couple of pillows. He got behind the couch and put them in the spots I kept landing on. Mum liked that idea and I guess I thought it was a good idea too. Those pillows looked a lot softer than the floor did and would certainly be more comfortable to land on.

Over the next few days, I made sure to do my part and remind my friends about our pay it forward birthday celebration. Mum kept most of my birthday packages that were coming in set aside and was making me wait until my actual birthday to open them. The night before my birthday she brought them all out and set them on the coffee table so I could see them all. I was excited but wondered how mum thought I was going to get any sleep that night with all of those exciting surprises sitting right there in front of me. I decided to play extra hard to try to get worn out and see if that would help me sleep.

That extra playing helped to tire me out enough to sleep. When I woke up I was still surprised and excited about the pile of presents. Mum gave me happy birthday luvins and told me to be patient. Mum and dad both had to work and they would let me open my presents later that evening. Ugh, I had more waiting to do?

Gramma came over and visited with me while mum and dad were at work. She gave me extra birthday luvins and made sure I got extra treats. She was shocked at all of the presents on the table too and she told me how much my friends must love me to be so kind and send them. Gramma helped the day go by quicker and before I knew it mum and dad were both home.

Mum made me a tuna surprise for dinner that I absolutely loved and gobbled right up. Once I was done with my business and dad had the blankets on the couch cleaned up and changed out mum started putting my presents on the couch for me to check out. She tried to get a picture of me with all of my presents but she couldn't possibly get them all in the picture. I had a wonderful time seeing what was inside of all of those boxes. I got so many different kinds of treats and lots and lots of feather toys.

Mum said I was in sensory overload and maybe she was right because I wanted to play with everything all at the same time. I wanted to try a treat from each and every bag too! I bounced back and forth between pouncing on new toys, chomping on new feathers and trying new treats. I did this all night long and I was still going strong when mum and dad decided they were ready for bed. Mum gathered up all of my treats and put them in the drawer so Grace wouldn't eat them all, but she left all of my toys where I could play with them.

After they went to bed and I finally got tired enough to slow down and relax, I took time to think about how many wonderful friends I had. I was so happy that I could be a part of their lives and help them remember to never give up and love life no matter what. My friends made me so happy and helped give me something to live for every day. They meant as much to me as I did to them and together I felt like we could handle anything life ever threw at us.

Chapter Eleven – One World

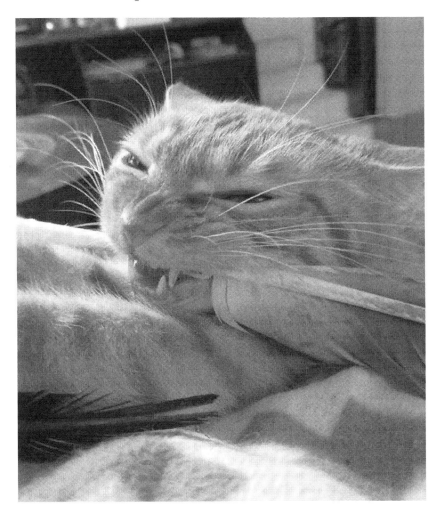

Neuro Dan - Feather Dan
June 4, 2016 ·

Hai my furiends. Iz had another good day. Mum opened another birthday present last night and it had FEATHERS in it! I got to get busy playing and chomping on one of them. Mum also took a video of me chomping and put it on something she called YouTube. Iz not sure what that's all about but she said if you click on the link you can watch the video if you want to. Hope everyone is having a good weekend. Iz getting back to chomping on my FEATHER again now. Sleep with the angels my friends. I luvs you.

I played hard that night and through the entire next day. When it finally got to be couch time and mum and dad came to sit down, I realized I had worn myself out. I still enjoyed some more treats and found enough energy to play for a while but I curled up and took a nap earlier than I normally would. When mum and dad got up to go to bed I woke up and got a notion.

One of my new presents was a super comfortable cat bed. It was the perfect size for me to curl up in and it was a perfect height to rest my chin on. Mum set it down by the glass door so when it was nice outside I'd have someplace to sit and watch the birds. I was in the mood for something different and it was still new, so I decided to check it out some more. I backed off the couch and made my way over to it. I got curled up in it and slept there for the entire night.

It turned out to be a great place to nap when I wanted a change from the Blankets Mountain scenery. Dad figured out why I liked it pretty quickly. He got up to get ready for work and saw me there. It was still dark when he got up but the sun came up before he left. As soon as the sun got above the tree line it covered the entire area by the glass door with giant warm sun puddles. I got to stretch out, soak up the sun and watch the birds catch their breakfast.

I sure did appreciate my friends. They just never knew how much of a difference they made in my life. The little cat bed was a perfect example. It gave me a new way to appreciate the beauty of the outside and allowed me to be comfortable while doing it. It helped keep things new for me and keep me stimulated. Mum always told me I was more intelligent than the average cat and she could see my mind working just by looking into my eyes. I didn't know about all of that but I did have more time to think about things than most other cats. I couldn't spend my awake time running around or climbing and jumping; instead I learned to enjoy studying everything, thinking and just simply living in the moment.

The cat bed in front of the glass door became another one of my favorite spots to hang out. I even got to say hi to outside cat, DJ, while I was there. Every morning dad would open up the glass door and fill up his food bowl. Sometimes DJ was out there waiting on dad and sometimes he was out on one of his adventures. When he was there I would stand up and tell him good morning. He would meow at dad and rub against his legs. Dad would give him some head scratches and come back inside.

Grace decided that she would come and lie down next to me in order to watch the outside too. Once she did that Amelia walked over to give her a bath and take a nap with her. Leroy would join us sometimes, but he would sprawl out on the floor behind us. Once the sun went up high enough that the sun puddles disappeared, Amelia would wander off and Grace would curl up in her usual spot in the middle of the living room. Leroy liked the bedroom more than any of the other rooms and spent most of the daytime in there.

Mum and dad both got used to seeing me resting in the new cat bed in the mornings. When I was on the floor, mum would make her cup of coffee and before she sat down at her desk, she would sit with me and give me luvins for a minute. When it was time for my breakfast, she would get it ready and carry me over to my feeding ledge. She would still help me get to my bathroom spot after I was done eating, and then she'd set me on Blankets Mountain.

She started a new routine. Since she couldn't tell right away if I wanted to be on Blankets Mountain or my cat bed she would wait for me to decide. If I wanted to be on Blankets Mountain I'd just curl up and make myself comfortable. If I wanted to be on my cat bed I'd either start working on getting down from the ledge or I would stand there and stare at the cat bed on the floor. Then I would look at mum and back at the cat bed. She would take me to the cat bed when I decided I wanted to go there. Sometimes I wanted both and I would stay on Blankets Mountain for a while. Then I would get myself down and go to the cat bed later. I was getting pretty good at climbing off the couch. It was still a challenge to get back up, but as long as my steps were there I could manage pretty well.

Oops, I forgot to tell you about my steps! Patti, one of mum's very good friends who she met because of me, sent me an Amazon package one day. It was a large, firm piece of foam what was shaped into about 5 steps. This made it so much easier to get onto the couch. It was nearly irreplaceable.

I guess it was the change of routines; being in different places and walking across the floor more often that started to get Amelia a little frisky. Every now and then she saw see me making my way to the cat bed and would come over and try to play. I really wanted to be able to play with her but I couldn't play the way she could. Sometimes it was frustrating for me and I am sure she felt the same way.

One morning she was trying a little too hard to get me to do the zoomies. Leroy happened to be walking by and he saw what was going on. I might have a hard time doing zoomies but that's one of Leroy's favorite games. He quietly hopped up on the couch, crouched, did vigorous butt wiggle and pounced. He leapt over the coffee table and landed right on top of her. He gave her quite the scare and she started hissing and spitting.

The hissing woke Grace up from her nap. She had been sleeping on the floor right next to us and she jumped to her feet with a muffled bark. Leroy realized what he'd done and ran away as fast as he could. He got past Grace before she could get a fix on either of them. He made it around the corner and into the bedroom, but Amelia wasn't quite as lucky. She was still recovering from Leroy's ambush, and since she didn't think she'd done anything to get cop dog after her, she didn't try to get away. Grace must have thought that she was hissing at me because she barked, took two fast steps, stuck her nose under Amelia's belly and rolled her over.

Eyes wide with surprise, Amelia tried to get her feet back under her to get away, but Grace kept rolling her across the living room until she got her up against the glass door. Amelia wound up with a belly covered in dog drool as Grace gave her sloppy licks. I stayed put and just hunkered down until the commotion was done. Amelia managed to get away and jump up onto mum's desk where she proceeded to give herself a bath.

Mum had been getting ready for work when the commotion started. She came around the corner with a toothbrush in her mouth, surveyed the situation and told everyone to settle it down. Grace went back to her favorite spot in the middle of the living room and walked in circles a few times before she curled up to resume her nap. I had almost made it to the cat bed so I completed the journey and made myself comfortable. Amelia spent a while on mum's desk trying to get her fur right again.

Mum came back out and was moving pretty quick. I hadn't gotten my breakfast yet but I knew when mum was moving that fast it meant she didn't have time to feed me. I was excited because that guaranteed me a lunch date with gramma! I was right. Mum grabbed her purse and gave me goodbye luvins. When she did she told me to be sure to eat good for gramma.

A couple hours later I heard the door unlock. Grace did her usual thing and charged the door barking the entire time. The barking stopped and I could hear her tail smacking the wall in the hallway. Gramma was laughing and telling her to calm down. She came around the corner and when I saw her, I stood up and gave her a big smile to say hello. Leroy and Amelia came running and we all got our treats. Then she went into the kitchen and made my lunch. She scooped me up and took me to my ledge and we had a nice lunch date. I ate really well for her too. She didn't always give us treats before I got lunch. I didn't want her to think it spoiled my appetite, so I ate really well for her. That made her happy and we got another round of treats before she left.

When mum left, she let dad know she was running late and wasn't going to have time to feed me but she forgot to tell him that gramma said she could help out. By the time dad got home he figured I was starving so before he even took Grace out for her walk, he set a handful of treats down on Blankets Mountain for me. I had them almost all gone by the time he got back in.

He hurried into the kitchen and got my dinner ready. Since I'd had a late lunch I wasn't quite as hungry as I usually would have been by that time of the evening. As a result I didn't eat very well for him. He got worried and went to the desk drawer and got out some of the special treats. I gave him my big eyes and that got me two special treats! He called mum and told her he was worried because I hadn't eaten my dinner. When mum told him that was because I got a late lunch he was relieved and laughed because he realized I'd gotten away with bonus treats. He didn't mind; he just sat with me and gave me luvins while he chuckled.

I got a good laugh later that night. All of those extra treats made me gassy. I had to admit they were pretty potent and mum and dad got up and ran away a few times. Every time they jumped up and made funny noises while waving their hands in front of their faces, Grace would get confused. She would jump up and start whining. The potent gas might have distracted dad from extra feathers play, but the way they kept getting up and fanning their faces made me laugh so I didn't mind.

The next day mum decided to go outside. There were some new flowers that had bloomed and she thought they were pretty and wanted to take a closer look. She stopped and asked me if I wanted to go smell the flowers with her. I gave her a big smile and stood up. She scooped me up and out we went. The flowers were right around the corner. They were blue with speckles of white and I thought they smelled nice. I thought mum was going to pluck one and take it inside. She must have read my mind because she told me they were meant to be outside flowers and if we brought any in, Leroy would probably try to eat them.

Mum walked us around for a little while and I enjoyed soaking up the sun. It was always exciting to see different things when I went outside. This time, I got to see some birds flying around in the trees. DJ came around too and he rolled around on his back in the sun. Mum let us sniff noses which was something I'd wanted to do for a long time. He smelled of the outdoors. He smelled friendly too.

I couldn't figure out why he would never come inside. I guess I could understand when there were nice sunny days like this when all of the pretty flowers were out and birds were chirping. It wasn't so nice and sunny out here all the time though. There were plenty of times when we got terrible thunder boomers and it got really cold during the winter. DJ never complained although we all wished he would just come in.

It was a hot day and Mum decided we'd been outside long enough. We came back in to cool off and mum sat down with me on the couch. She had her laptop out and was looking at my Facebook page. She read some more of the comments and replied to a few questions. She was looking at a tool Facebook had for their page managers that was called "Insights." She then looked at me and asked me if I knew I had friends from forty five different countries. I had no idea but I was pretty shocked. My friends truly did come from all over the world! She told me each country everyone came from and I was very surprised at some of them. I was humbled and grateful to be loved by so many people.

Mum told me that I was a very special boy to be able to speak to the hearts of people from all over the entire world. She said that it just showed that no matter where we are from we are all more alike than not. I understood that very well. I knew that everyone could feel love and that sometimes everyone also needed to be encouraged. I hoped that I could help others understand that despite different cultures and beliefs; it was possible for all of our different cultures on this planet to get along and live in peace.

Later that night while dad was playing with me, I started to get another notion. It had been a little while since I surprised mum or dad with one of my floor adventures. I was feeling frisky, so I started to come up with an idea for the next morning. I stayed on Blankets Mountain that night and thought things over. After my breakfast the next morning I decided to tell mum to let me stay on Blankets Mountain.

Once she sat down at her desk to start getting ready I snuck off the couch. I stayed hidden behind the coffee table as I made my way across the living room. I managed to sneak around the side of her desk and slip between it and the glass door. I knew she heard the blinds clatter a little. She must have thought it was Leroy or Amelia because she didn't even look. I got under her desk and made my way over to her feet. I got up on my back legs, stretched my front legs up and put my front feet on her legs. She looked down expecting to see Leroy and when she saw me I could tell by the look on her face that I managed to surprise her. I knew that would do it! It also got me picked up and snuggled with while she finished getting ready.

Mum had a short work day and was home really early. She cleaned up around the house for a little while, but she kept looking at her phone. I was sitting on the floor looking outside and watching her bustle about. She came and sat down next to me to give me some luvins. She looked at her phone one more time then asked me if she should take her free time to help some other kitties. I gave her my best big eyed happy look to let her know that, yes; I did think she should go help some kitties if she could.

She told me there was a litter of kittens that were abandoned on the side of the road. Someone had rescued them but they couldn't keep them. There was a dog rescue who had volunteered to take them in until a better suited placement could be found but they couldn't go get them. They were asking across Facebook for someone to help with the transport. Mum told me I was right and of course she should help if she could. She replied to them and in just a few minutes later she was talking on the phone with someone. She gave me a kiss and out the door she went.

She got home later than normal that night, but she sure had a big smile on her face. She said the kittens were absolutely adorable and she wished she could have just taken them all home with her. Dad gave her a funny look and she promised him she hadn't. They were safe for the moment but the rescue that had taken them was for dogs and they were hoping to find another place quickly.

The next day they found out that the kittens had turned out to be FIV positive. I wasn't really sure what it meant but I'd heard about it before when I was at Misfits and I knew it could be a problem. The dog rescue had to get them moved as quickly as they could. Mum shared the story with my Facebook friends and over the next couple of days they all came together to try to find someplace for them to go. The story was shared enough that the kittens were taken in by another rescue that dealt with FIV positive animals. I was so happy that it worked out for them! They reminded me of my own life and how lucky I had been in my beginning. I was very proud of all of the people who were so willing to give of themselves to help animals in need.

Chapter Twelve – The Month of Booms

Neuro Dan - Feather Dan

· July 27, 2016 ·

Hai my furiends. Mum is back on her computer finishing up her reports for work but its FEATHERS and treats time. Iz got to find a way to get her attention so I can get some of these Temptations. Iz sure if I make enough noise she'll come check on me, otherwise I'll have to go on an adventure and go fetch her myself. Sleep with the angels tonight my friends. I luvs you all.

The next weekend dad decided it was time to clean out and organize the storage closet on the porch. I stayed back on the couch and watched him work. I was surprised at how many boxes he kept pulling out and stacking up. He came in and out several times. Sometimes he grabbed more garbage bags and sometimes he took small items from the boxes inside and set them on his desk.

I studied every movement he made and it was paying off. I noticed that every now and then when he opened the door a small moth or other insect would fly inside with him. So far I saw three moths' that had come in and landed on the ceiling. Neither Leroy nor Amelia had seen them yet and I wondered how long it would take for them to notice. The moths didn't move at all and they would be difficult for Leroy and Amelia to spot until they started to fly around.

Dad finally got done and after he got cleaned up he got me my dinner. Mum got home and he showed her some things he'd pulled out of the totes. Mum said it was a little walk down memory lane. I liked the sound of that. I wondered how I could get mum to go back and look at some of the old pictures from when I first got here. That memory lane experience sounded like a good time.

After we sat down for couch time, those moths started to fly around. I was keeping an eye on them and one of them kept getting closer and closer. Then I got surprised by another bug that I didn't notice sneak in. It flew past my right ear so close that it tickled me! When it zipped in front of me, I got a really good look at it. I could not believe what I was seeing. Its butt lit up and glowed! Whoa! How did the bugs butt turn on and off like a light? I didn't see any switches on it. Dad saw it too and chuckled at the expression on my face. Mum and dad watched it fly all the way over towards dad's desk and land on the wall.

I had forgotten about the moths after I got buzzed by the bug with the blinking butt. They must have started flying around again though because I heard Amelia chattering up a storm in the kitchen. I hopped up on the couch cushion and looked over. There she was chasing after one of the moths' that had flown low enough to get her attention.

It gained some altitude but flew towards the kitchen table. Amelia jumped up on the table and swatted furiously at it. It stayed just out of her range and kept on going. She jumped as high as she could and she bopped it but didn't knock it out of the sky. She did manage to knock over everything that was on the kitchen table; except for the food bowl of course.

Leroy heard the commotion and came trotting out of the bedroom. Grace gave a bark once things started getting knocked down and ran into the kitchen to investigate. The bug kept on going and was flying higher and going towards a display case. Amelia looked like she was about to jump up on top of the display case and dad fussed at her. There were old lanterns and other antiques on top of it that he didn't want her to break.

She didn't listen to dad so he snapped his fingers. That got Grace's attention and she looked at him. She got a real hard eyed and focused look when dad gave her commands. Mum always said she got that look when she felt like she was working and she really liked to work. Dad pointed at Amelia and told Grace "Bad Kitty!" That was all Grace needed to hear. She barked, hopped up and landed with her front feet on the table. She made a silly snarling noise, made one more hop and grabbed Amelia by the back of her leg. She gently pulled her across the table and when she was close enough she used her nose to knock her down.

Dad gave Grace one more command and Amelia started to run. She didn't have a head start so she didn't have a chance. Grace got her with the pit maneuver and crashed her into the garbage can. Grace always did an extra thorough job of the pit maneuver when dad gave her the command. When she was just keeping the peace around the house she would use just one pit maneuver, drool on the belly and be done. When dad gave her the command, it was pit maneuver after pit maneuver until they couldn't escape. The only upside to it was she didn't take time to give wet bellies.

She let Amelia get up and take two steps before she executed another pit maneuver on her. She got the pit maneuver three more times before she managed to get to the cat tree and climb to the high ground. Grace sat at the bottom of the cat tree and stared at her. Once she had the command she'd keep it up until she got the command to stop. Dad told her to stop and told her she was a good girl. He got up, gave her some petting and pats on the side. He walked to his desk to get her a brand new bone. He told her to sit and when she did, he gave her the bone. She jumped and bounced around happy as could be before she sat down. She was extra vigorous when she started chewing on that bone. Of course, dad also walked over to the cat tree to give Amelia some words of encouragement and chin scritches.

Those moths got chased after and provided entertainment for a few days before they finally just stopped showing up. I don't know where they went. One day they were there and then one night they just weren't. Amelia in particular liked those moths and she kept looking for them for days. She would spend hours just staring at the ceiling, waiting for one to appear. She finally either forgot or gave up and went back to her normal routine of napping.

Mum had a friend come over and visit. Her friend had some children with her. I got to meet them and they seemed nice. I was patient and let them pet me and say hi. One of them really liked me and wanted to know if he could take me home. When mum said no he went and played with Leroy and then wanted to know if he could take him home. Mum said no again and he asked if he could take Amelia home. Mum had to explain to him that this was their home and they would be sad if they had to leave.

He understood and all of them left. Before they left they had changed into some different looking clothes and they were talking about going to play in a swimming pool. I couldn't believe mum was going to go and voluntarily get in a big hole with water in it! What was she thinking? I understood that they had to take showers but those were over pretty quick. I thought they were nuts wanting to go and actually splash around in a pool. It would take them forever to get their fur right and their clothes would be soaked.

They were gone for a couple of hours and when they got back mum looked funny. Not only was her hair all wet but she had turned a funny color of red. I didn't know people could just turn funny colors like that. I hadn't seen her do that before and I was fascinated. Her friend and the children came back in and everyone got changed back into normal clothes. Before her friend left she rubbed something mum called aloe all over her back and shoulders. I heard her say that she was going to be hurting soon.

When dad got home he took one look at her and I could tell he felt bad for her. He asked her how in the world she had managed to get that mean looking sunburn. Mum told him about going to the pool with her friend and the kids. Dad asked her if she had anything to put on it and she told him about the aloe. He said that was just another reason he didn't care for going to pools. I agreed with dad. I didn't think it made any sense at all to go get all wet and then come back burned up too.

Poor mum was starting to get sore and grouchy before the night was over. Dad put that aloe stuff on her several times over the next few days. Near the end of the week mums skin started to come off! I was shocked! She was looking at her burn that had been healing and the next thing I knew she was pulling a great big piece of her skin right off her shoulder. Holy Cat! Mum was literally falling apart! Her face looked like it was riddled with white, dry skin.

When dad got home she told him she started peeling. Dad didn't look surprised at all that mum was pulling her skin off. I was pretty confused about the entire situation. I think it was time I had a serious talk with mum about the pool. I didn't think it was a good idea for her to go back there if she was going to start coming apart afterwards.

Mum and dad started talking about a holiday that was coming up. I got excited because I like the holidays and traditions. It always means there is some good food and I get a little bite of whatever they make. Plus it usually means the house is going to smell really yummy for at least one day.

Mum asked me if I remembered the Fourth of July. I had to think about it but yes I did. It was my least favorite of all of the holidays. That holiday there were always loud bangs that went on for an entire night. I wondered if we still had the same neighbors who, last year, started blowing things up a couple of days before the fourth. Those loud noises stressed me out bad. Even Grace who normally charged at anything didn't like those and would go hide under the bed.

Mum asked my Facebook friends that night if any of them had any suggestions for how to deal with the noise. Some of them said to turn the television volume up extra high. One person said they could turn on music and sing to their kitties and that helped. It seemed like most people were in the same position with their pets. At least I knew I wasn't the only one who got scared over those loud noises and that made me feel a little better.

We got the final numbers back for that project that Clovis and I had collaborated with to celebrate our birthdays. We were able to raise enough money to help both rescues make a huge difference in their communities. I was so proud of all of my friends for being willing to help out. That meant there would be more kitties being rescued from animal control and brought into no-kill shelters. Each one of those kitties would have a chance to find their forever homes and that just meant the world to me.

The next day we had neighbors start firing off those loud fireworks. The first one scared all of us terribly. We heard a small pop followed by an earie whistling sound that went on for a few seconds. When the whistling went quiet the entire neighborhood shook with the bang that followed. It was immediately followed up by a second one.

Before the second one went off Leroy had sprinted from the guest bedroom and shot into the main bedroom. Grace barked at the glass door and the hackles on her neck were standing up. She looked extra vicious when those hackles got up and that only happened when she meant serious business. Amelia leapt out of mum's desk chair so fast that it was spinning in circles. She was right behind Leroy on her way to the bedroom.

The first boom got me on my feet. My heart was racing and I was trying to figure out what to do. The second boom made me jump and I started to get down off of Blankets Mountain. The booms kept coming. First a little pop, whistle noise, and then BOOM! Even the windows shook. I barely made it to my bathroom spot to do my business but I did and when I was done I decided to get off the couch completely. I still didn't know where to go but the booms were nonstop.

Grace was mad and still barking at the glass door. The neighbors behind our apartments in the house right behind us and down a small hill were the ones firing them off. They were exploding above the trees right in front of our porch. I could see the glass shake every time one exploded. Different kinds of bangs started to happen and Grace gave a funny sounding bark, turned and ran into the bedroom. She was still barking every time a firework went off but her barks were muffled which meant she had hidden under the bed.

I made it to the ground but didn't know where to go. I wished either mum or dad were home but they weren't and I had to figure it out on my own. As the explosions kept coming I decided I would take shelter under mum's desk. I crawled all the way to the back corner and hid my head against the corner of the wall.

A few minutes later and I heard the front door open. Gramma had come to check on us and she called for Grace and started looking for me. It took her a minute to find me but when she did she got down on her hands and knees and crawled under mum's desk with me. I was quivering when she got to me and she pet me for a minute then scooped me up and carried me back to the couch. She set me on Blankets Mountain and stayed with me giving me comfort.

Grace came out from the bedroom. Her head was hanging and tail was down and not wagging. She whined as she came up and laid her head in grammas lap. Gramma stroked Grace's head with one hand and mine with the other. She sat with us for an hour while we waited for the neighbors to stop launching the fireworks. She sang soothing songs that helped us take our minds off the horrific noises outside. Gramma then called mum and told her what had been going on.

I could hear mum on the other end of the phone and whoa was she mad. When she got home that night she put up what dad called a "rant" on my Facebook page. She was very upset about the neighbors starting up with the fireworks so early. She knew we would have to deal with it when the holiday was officially celebrated and she had already made plans to be home to help us through it. She hadn't expected that we'd be terrorized for days prior to the official celebration. She was mostly concerned about my neurological condition because extreme stress could cause me to have immediate and permanent progression of my disease, which could significantly shorten my lifespan. She knew the neighbors didn't mean any harm and were only trying to have fun, but she was upset by what it did to us.

The next couple of days were pretty hard on me. I think the neighbors had taken the entire week off because the explosions started and stopped randomly all day for two days straight. The day that our town had decided they were going to celebrate finally came and mum had the day off. She stayed home and sat with us. The neighbors kept on making a racket and I was starting to get used to it. I wasn't trying to hide under mum's desk anymore and I finally stopped shaking. Mum could look at me tell I was really mad and that got her all worked up again.

Mum and dad were both home when the country club that was close to the apartments had their fireworks performance. It was loud and there sure were a lot of booms. It felt like it went on for a really long time. It wasn't nearly as bad as the neighbors' booms though. Those booms were happened right above us and below us. At least the country club's booms were a little farther off. When they finally completed their finale, the neighbors decided to have a grand finale of their own.

We were all grateful when it was over with. The next day, I was so tired from being so stressed that I just slept. I didn't even want to play with my feathers but I did enjoy getting my luvins from mum and dad. Leroy and Amelia finally came back out of the bedroom. They had been in hiding almost the entire time. The only time I saw them sneak out was to go use the litter box or get something to eat. Grace got back to her normal self almost immediately. She never stayed bothered by much once whatever was upsetting her stopped. I would try to learn from her and just relax. She knew how to live in the moment, and after such a stressful week that's exactly what I needed to be reminded of. I took a breath and just enjoyed the luvins I was getting from mum and dad.

Over the next couple of weeks things got back to normal. Mum was taking some more college classes and her new schedule meant that I was getting a lot more lunch dates with gramma. I looked forward to each one. I got used to hearing her key unlock the door and her saying hi when she came in. I always stood up to greet her and gave her the biggest smiles I could. I started giving her my best wet faced mushes too. One day I made her extra happy and rolled over and let her pet my belly. I only let mum and dad pet my belly, but gramma was making me so happy I started letting her do it too. I don't know why, but that made her happier than I have seen her in a long time.

One day we had such a bad thunderstorm that the noise it was making was putting those fireworks to shame. Gramma must have known that the storm was coming because she had already come over and fed me earlier than normal. All of a sudden, the loudest noise I ever heard boomed once and almost immediately after, boomed again.

The entire building shook so hard that a couple of pictures fell off the walls. Grace barked for a few seconds then started whining and running back and forth across the house. She was running from the bedroom through the living room and down the hall to the front door. She would then turn around and do it again. She kept whining and pacing back and forth, which had me confused. I never saw her act like that before.

Then I heard a noise I'd heard before, but it kept getting closer and closer. The noise was the sirens of, what I knew from listening to mum and dad, were firetrucks. They sounded like they stopped right next to our building. I could hear all kinds of yelling and other sounds I couldn't identify. Then our front door opened up, and in ran gramma. She was soaking wet from having run across the parking lot in the storm.

She saw me sitting on Blankets Mountain and looked relieved. She rushed into the guest bedroom and came out with my cat carrier. She ran over to me, scooped me up and plopped me in my carrier. She zipped it up and set me down next to the front door. She went back in the guest bedroom and came out with another cat carrier and started calling for Leroy and Amelia. Neither of them would come out. I was pretty sure they were hiding up inside the box spring under mum and dads bed. That was where they would go hide if things got too scary.

When they didn't come out, for the first time ever, I heard gramma say a word I should have covered my ears for. She grabbed Graces leash and hooked her up. She grabbed my carrier and rushed us out the front door. She ran up the steps and when we got to the parking lot, I could see three fire trucks with firefighters dragging hoses and shooting giant streams of water into our apartment building. Right next to our front sidewalk I saw what was left of a tree that had been there.

Lightning had struck our building and the tree. The tree was smoldering and broken in half. The far side of our building had flames coming of the top apartment. The firefighters were doing a good job though and it looked like they had it under control. Gramma started to take us to her apartment in the building across the parking lot but one of the firefighters stopped her and told her we would be safe. He told her that they contained it to just one apartment so there was no danger for us on our side of the building.

Gramma breathed a big sigh of relief. The rain had stopped so she stood there with me and Grace and watched as they finished putting out the fire. A pretty big crowd had gathered to watch and I thought it was neat to see so many new people. She heard the firefighters talking and they said that one unit was a total loss and the apartments below it had some pretty serious water damage but the building was structurally sound.

When the firefighters got back in their trucks and left, she took me and Grace back downstairs to our apartment. She put me back on Blankets Mountain, and then took Grace out to do her business. When she came back in she was on the phone with mum. She let mum know what happened and that everything was fine. She told mum to make sure to let dad know too because she had already seen people posting on Facebook about the fire and she didn't want him to be worried.

I felt really sad for the families that had lost everything in the fire. Mum and dad talked about it and they were glad that having insurance was mandatory in order to live there. They found out later that those families didn't have any pets and that made all of us feel even better knowing no animals or people had been hurt. Dad told mum that gramma was a hero for rushing over to save us. She had planned on getting me and Grace to her apartment and coming back to try to get Leroy and Amelia too. When she realized that they were going to be okay, she went down to comfort them.

Gramma was like a superhero. She was always there when mum or dad couldn't be. She made sure I never missed a meal. She went with mum when I had to go to the vets anytime she was asked. Now she was even running into burning buildings to rescue us. That was pretty impressive and I thought maybe she deserved to have a costume with a cape. She didn't need a mask like some of those superheroes had though because I thought she was very pretty and had no reason to hide her face. Even though it had been a scary day I slept good that night knowing that gramma would be there if mum or dad couldn't.

Chapter Thirteen –Slappy-Paws

Neuro Dan - Feather Dan August 25, 2016 ·

Hai my furiends. Iz been extra snuggly today and since mum was home I got lotz of lovin. I even got upside down belly rubs. Now I got lotz of energy and itz FEATHERS time. Dad sayz itz also football time. I guess football must be like FEATHERS for dad because he gets real excited. Good thing dad can watch football and play FEATHERS at the same time. That means I don't have to hide the remote. Sleep with the angels tonight my friends. I luvs you all.

I was starting to feel pretty brave. We'd had fireworks, terrible thunder boomers, the apartment even caught on fire and we were all still here and okay. When mum got out the vacuum that weekend, instead of asking her to take me to another room, I thought I would just show her how brave I was by staying on Blankets Mountain. Mum sure was surprised and she told me that being that brave would get me extra treats.

Amelia must have been starting to feel more brave too because that night when I was playing with my feathers she tried to sneak up on me. She was crouching on floor at the foot of the couch below me. She didn't think I noticed her but I'm pretty good about staying alert and knowing exactly what's going on around me. I kept an eye on her while she started trying to sneak a paw over the couch to snatch a feather.

She finally got her claws hooked into one of my big goose feathers and slowly started to pull it over the edge of the couch. I made her jump when I spun around and pounced on the feather. She pulled her paw back because she was startled, but tried to reach back up for it again. I was thinking that maybe she wanted to play a game of slappy-paws so I pounced on her paw too. She hissed and pulled her paw back but didn't run away.

I popped my head over the couch. I gave her one of my sideways head cocked looks to see what her intentions were. This time, she didn't hiss at me, she kept staring at the feather. I figured I had plenty of feathers at the moment and I never minded sharing as long as I still had feathers to play with. I gave the feather a little nudge towards the edge. She saw it pop out over her head and swatted it. She knocked it to the ground, grabbed it by its stem and ran away to the cat tree. She played with it over there for quite a while before she took a nap.

The next day I started not being very hungry during the mornings. I started getting picky and eating much slower than normal. Mum, dad and gramma all tried different things to see if they could figure out what I wanted. It wasn't that I wanted a different food I just wasn't feeling very hungry. I ate great for dinner every night so mum wasn't concerned about me missing out on calories but she told everyone to keep her updated about how much I ate in the mornings. She was worried I might get dehydrated and said she'd take me in to the vet for IV fluids if she thought I needed it.

Everyone knows that Leroy just loves boxes. He'll do anything to be able to get into a box. Mum got something in the mail and it had a medium sized box that he could squeeze into, but his back legs would hang out. She set it down in the kitchen next to the garbage can for dad to take out when he had a chance. She also tossed a couple of grocery bags that had holes in them into the box to go out too.

Later that day, Leroy started rooting around in the box and the next thing we knew he was making a racket. Somehow, he managed to slip his head through the bags handle and was wearing it like a cape. When he tried to walk it touched his tail and spooked him. He jumped and started to run, but the bag turned and he got his legs caught in it and fell over. The noise got Grace up and barking as she went to check him out. He saw Grace come around the couch and tried to jump up on the couch to get mum to help him but his legs were still tangled. Instead of his normal leaping-Leroy jump, he wound up hitting the side of the couch. Dad told Grace to leave him alone and Leroy walked over in front of mum to show her his predicament. He then gave her a pathetic 'help me' look. She got the bag off and he went back to playing in the box. From that day on,

Mum made sure all the handles on the grocery bags were cut before throwing them out.

Leroy's antics got me feeling frisky and I wound up getting a notion. Mum and dad both left really early for work the next day and I knew that meant I was going to get another lunch date with gramma. I decided I was going to find somewhere else to hide and see how she did with the game of hide and seek. I figured I better look around for a fun place.

I started to walk from Blankets Mountain across the back of the couch. It was easier to find a hiding spot if I was higher up because that was the view gramma would have. I got to the turn in L-shaped couch and followed the wall towards where I played feathers. I looked over the edge and behind the couch and spotted the pillows dad put down back there in case I pulled another superman and jumped off the back.

I stopped and looked around for a minute. I then decided I wanted to try to get on mums desk chair. Amelia liked to sleep there a lot, so I knew it would be a comfortable place to hide until gramma got here. I got to the edge of the couch and started to make my way down to the end table where I planned on walking over to mums chair. That was when I accidentally slipped and wound up falling behind the couch again. I'd gone farther than I normally do and was past where dad had put the last pillow. I managed to land on my feet but it sure didn't feel good. I decided that I was going to just rest there for a while and recover. While I was resting, I figured that this was probably a pretty good hiding spot anyway so I just stayed put.

When gramma showed up she couldn't find me anywhere. She stayed calm and looked in my usual spots but, when she still couldn't find me she got frantic. She looked for over ten minutes before she spotted me. I was just relaxing but poor gramma thought I was hurt and got scared. That was when I discovered that gramma has superhuman strength! Did you know that gramma can pick up a great big sectional couch all by herself? Me neither but she sure did! She picked up that big heavy couch all by herself and dragged it far enough away from the wall that she could walk behind it.

She hurried back there and got me. She put me on Blankets Mountain and sat with me. She was trying to make sure I was okay and nothing was hurt. I felt bad that she was so worried so I stood up and walked in a circle; then gave her a wet faced mush on her nose and glasses to make sure she knew I was fine. I think she felt better after that because she walked to the kitchen and made my lunch. Once my lunch was done she looked at the couch. She went behind it and picked up the pillows that dad put on the floor, and set them on the couch. Then she put her hands on the couch, took a deep breath and pushed on it until it started to move. She grunted and pushed it all the way to the wall. She kept pushing until she couldn't see any light between the couch and wall. There was no way I could ever fall behind it again.

I still wasn't eating much during breakfasts, but I still ate my dinner and I was always full of energy. I went on another floor adventure for two more days in a row. I was playing extra hard with my feathers at night too. Mum kept checking on my pee pads and she did weird things like pinching my skin to make sure I was staying hydrated. I was also getting some liquid kitty yogurt treats at night and I loved it.

One day mum forgot to tell gramma that her classes had been canceled and she would be home to feed me. Gramma showed up for our regular lunch date and was surprised to see mum. They talked for a minute and gramma did what she always does. She went and said hi to Leroy and Amelia, then came over and gave me snuggles.

She told mum she would just feed me anyway since she was there. I gave her good wet face mushes and even made sure to smear her glasses so she knew I loved her lots.

When she sat down to feed me I kept turning my head when she put food in front of me. I had been hoping for a treat before I got my lunch and then some extras for dessert afterwards. Gramma knew what I wanted, so she finally got up and went to mums desk. She got me one of those good beef stick treats and gave me a few bites of it. She told me I couldn't have the rest until I ate my lunch. I thought that was fair so I went ahead and ate half my lunch. Gramma finished giving me my beef stick treat and mum laughed at her. Mum told gramma that I had her trained. I wasn't so sure about that. I just think gramma loves me.

I got another package in the mail and it was one of those long tubes that always come with feathers. Mum opened it up and she pulled out a note and two giant beautiful peacock feathers! She read the note and told me that the feathers were from one of my friends. That friend has a pet peacock named Rupert Poppycock. Well my friend Rupert said he was done with those two feathers and has lots more for himself, so he sent those to me. That was really nice of him!

Mum and dad both got home early that day. Dad was impressed with the size of the peacock feathers too. He decided to sit down early and play with me. When he saw how excited I was and how hard I was playing he also decided to take some videos of me. I didn't mind the videos I was having too much fun playing. Plus I knew that if I cooperated with the camera I'd be sure to get extra treats. I had mum send Rupert a message to say thank you because that was one super fun day.

I played with those peacock feathers for days. Dad was having fun with them too. He could play with both of them at once and I'd go crazy trying to decide which one to pounce on. I would pick one, pounce it, then bite it and hold on tight. Then I would find the other one and pounce on it with the first one still in my mouth. They were long so he could get them to dance high up in the sky and I had fun stalking them when he would try to hide them behind the pillows.

Gramma came over for our lunch date one afternoon and she brought a laundry basket full of clothes with her. I gave her a funny look because I wasn't sure what laundry baskets had to do with lunch dates. She looked at me and told me her washer was broken and she was going to get a load done for her and gramma-great here because it was still going to be a couple of days before their new one was installed. I sure didn't mind that one bit. She stayed for an extra-long time and I got more treats than ever. She even played with me and the peacock feathers. That was when I decided that maybe she should just do her laundry here all the time.

The next day me and mum both had a bad day. I started having some increased neurological issues and wasn't in the mood to do anything. Mum came down with what she called a summer cold. I wasn't sure how she could get a cold because it was really nice outside, but she obviously didn't feel well. Mum told dad to let me have extra treats until I started feeling better because they were like chicken soup for me when I wasn't feeling good. I told dad he should give mum some of them too if he thought they would help her feel better.

The next day, my neurological issues started to clear up and I felt good enough to play with my feathers. There had been a big change in temperature and humidity over the last couple of days and any significant weather changes tended to make my condition act funny. I made up for the lack of play time from the night before and got in some great feather chomping that night.

I was listening to mum and dad talk that night and they were talking about gramma. Gramma was going out of town for a week to help mums sister with something in Florida. Mum and dad were trying to figure out which one of them would be able to get me food on which days. I knew that meant I was going to be eating much earlier than I liked to. I already didn't have much of an appetite in the mornings so I wasn't sure how this was going to work. I didn't worry about it too much though. The worse thing that would happen is I would be hungry for a little while before dinner, but then I knew I was sure to get extra treats. I also bet that I would get all the special occasion treats too. They finally got my feeding schedule figured out and I managed to do okay. Since I already wasn't eating much for lunch, I wound up just eating about the same amount for breakfast.

One of those days, mum got the day off and things were pretty normal. I was in the mood for extra snuggles and mum likes it when that happens. We spent the day snuggling and I even got lots of good belly rubs. By the time dad got home I was full of energy and ready for feathers. It turned out that dad's favorite sport was starting back up that night. Both mum and dad were pretty happy that it was football season again.

I remembered last year and all the traditions that came with football season, so I started getting excited too. That meant that Sundays were going to be super fun again. Dad would sit with me all day and I'd get extra treats every time something good happened with the team he was cheering for. I also knew that meant I'd smell those chicken wings again. They smelled so good, but mum always told me they were too hot for me and I wouldn't like them.

Dad was good at watching football and playing with feathers at the same time. I knew I wouldn't have to hide the remote on him to get his attention. The next night when dad turned the channel to football, mum started to grumble at him. She said something about it only being a preseason game and she didn't want to watch all of them. I thought mum was about to take the remote away from dad, but in the end they figured out a way to make them both happy. They decided to go back and forth between a football game and a show mum was interested in. When the game played, mum would pet me and give me ear rubs. When her show was playing, dad broke out the feathers. I got the best of both worlds and could not have been any happier than I was right then.

Neuro Dan - Feather Dan
September 28, 2016 ·

Hai my furiends. I hope everyone is having a good week. I had a quiet day today. Mum and dad both had to work so I got lots of naps and am well rested. Now Iz ready for FEATHERS time! Yup, all that rest got me frisky and now I declare it FEATHERS time. And Temptations time too, and maybe even beef stick time. And let's not forget belly rubs time right before bed. Yup, sounds like a good night to me. Sleep with the angels tonight my friends. I luvs you all.

The next day I woke up and my left eye was swollen, red and leaky. Mum noticed it right away and spent a minute checking it out. She said she was going to call my vet as soon as they opened and take me in to get it checked out. Well, having a swollen, leaky eye didn't mean I wasn't full of energy. I could still see just fine out of my right eye so I decided to go on a floor adventure. My cat bed was in the wash the day before, so dad set up a small pile of blankets in front of the glass door for me to lie on.

I climbed down Blankets Mountain and backed up over the edge of the couch. I only had to rest once on my way to the glass door. I managed to get comfortable just in time for the sun to come up and cover the floor in sun puddles. I soaked up the heat and watched the birds fly around until it was time for my breakfast. Mum called the vet and told me we would go as soon as I finished my breakfast.

It was a pretty good trip if you could say there was a good trip to the vets. My regular vet was in town so it was only a ten minute ride there. I didn't get poked or prodded. I didn't even have to get stuck with any needles! Everyone at the vets was happy to see me. I forgot that some of the workers there were fans and friends with me on my Facebook page. Mum and the vet knew each other for many years and they spent more time chatting and catching up than they did looking me over. The vet said it was just pink eye and he gave mum some eye drops that he said would clear it up in a few days.

Just like the vet said, it took a few days but my eye got better. Gramma made it back from her trip to Florida and finally stopped in for a visit. When she came in the door she was walking with sticks under her arms. Mum told me they were crutches. Gramma accidentally stubbed her foot on a table leg and broke some toes. She needed the crutches to help her walk. She was struggling with figuring them out and she looked like she was having a hard time getting around.

I certainly knew what it was like to have a hard time getting around. Mum told me I was going to be having a lunch date with gramma tomorrow. I decided I was going to have a talk with gramma then. I was going to give her some encouragement and explain to her that sometimes when you have a hard time walking, it's easier to just go slow and be patient. She would be better in no time, but I would make sure I did the best I could to cooperate with her during our lunch dates.

Sundays were back to being my favorite day of the week again. Dad really enjoyed watching those football games. I really enjoyed all the extra treats and luvins I got. Dad was doing that thing he called fantasy football again and I guess things were starting out pretty good for him. He was in a great mood by the end of the day. Last year, he won the whole game and got a jersey that was autographed by one of mum's favorite players. That made mum and dad both happy so he was trying for more prizes again this year.

Amelia was normally a classy lady. She always stayed groomed, sat proper and even with those big old polydactyl feet she walked proper. Every now and then, however, her inner mischievous cat would come out. One day, while mum and dad were both at work; she decided to be a stinker.

That morning, dad pulled a bag of trash out of the can but was running late and didn't have time to take it out. Usually if one of us is going to get into a bag of trash left lying around it was Grace. She would dig in there and look for anything that she thought might taste good. Personally, I don't understand why anyone would want to dig through some garbage when all you have to do is give mum the eyes and you get treats; but it seems to be something that others (mostly Grace) just can't seem to resist.

This time it was Amelia who decided she was going to go digging. I heard her get into it and I walked down the back of the couch to where dad usually sat so I could see what she was doing. She managed to push the bag over on its side and was in the process of dragging everything out of it. I told her she really shouldn't do that and that she'd get in big trouble if she got caught. Of course she pretended she didn't hear me and just kept on dragging stuff out of the bag. She was making an even bigger mess than Grace did when she started digging in the mess. Grace didn't usually empty the entire bag. She would knock some things out in the process, but she would stick her entire head in and pull out whatever she was after. Amelia had things strewn all over the place, even into the kitchen.

She should have listened to me. She was inside the bag and didn't hear when a key went into the front door and unlocked it. She didn't even hear it when dad opened up the door and walked in. She was so focused on what she was doing that she didn't even hear Grace run around the couch to greet dad. She sure did hear dad though when he caught her red handed and yelled at her. She scrambled out of the bag and ran for it. Dad didn't miss a beat though and he told Grace "bad kitty" and pointed at Amelia. Grace was excited about being given a job and chased Amelia down in earnest. She caught her before she could make the turn into the bedroom and gave her the pit maneuver.

Dad called Grace off but not before Amelia got a belly full of dog drool. Grace was proud of her good deed and wagged her tail as she waited for her praise. Dad went to his desk and gave her a new chew bone. He told her she was a very good girl and thanked her for her deed. Then he spent the next several minutes picking up a bag full of garbage while muttering under his breath words that were probably best that I couldn't understand. He took the trash out to the dumpster and I got luvins when he came back.

Amelia must have been in some crazy mood that day. She hadn't even gotten her belly cleaned up from all the dog drool when she came back out into the living room. She hopped up onto mums' desk and started snooping around. She didn't even care that dad was watching her; she grabbed one of mums hair ties and took off running with it. She ran over to the water bowl and dropped it right into the water. Dad asked her what the heck she was doing and she trotted back over to mums desk. She picked up another hair tie, ran back to the water bowl and dropped it in there too.

Dad was pretty exasperated. He asked her what was wrong with her but she started heading right back to mums desk again. Dad stood up and watched as she got a third hair tie. When she started trotting back to the water bowl again dad shook his head and called Grace. He told her "bad kitty" and pointed at Amelia again. Grace was extremely happy to be given a second job so quickly and she dropped her bone to charge straight at Amelia.

I don't think Amelia had any idea Grace was coming for her because she didn't even look behind her. Grace thrust her nose under her back legs and with a flip of her nose, sent Amelia spinning across the floor. She growled playfully as she kept pushing her with her nose, spinning her across the floor until she was pinned against a wall again. Amelia wound up with a wet belly for the second time in less than ten minutes.

That must have been enough for her because after dad called Grace off she ran back to the bedroom and didn't come out until after I had my dinner. When she did come out, it was because she heard the treat drawer open. I was getting my after-dinner treats and she was hoping she could get some too. I gave her a bewildered look and told her she probably wasn't going to have much luck getting treats from dad tonight, but maybe she could get some when mum got home.

Amelia was in a completely different mood the next day. She came over and snuggled with me on the couch for hours. She curled up beside me, gave me a few kisses and dozed off to sleep. She never comes up to snuggle with me. The closest she usually comes to snuggling is to sleep within a few feet of me or on the ledge above me if I'm on the cat tree. At first I thought she was up to something, but this time she wasn't. She was just in the mood to snuggle so I let her stay on the couch with me as long as she wanted to.

The next morning my neurological issues were acting up. I was having a hard time walking. When I went to do my business I wound up stumbling and made a big mess of myself. I knew I was in for a sink bath as soon as mum saw me and I was right. Mum overslept and got up later than she meant to. She was in a big hurry and didn't stop to tell me good morning right away. I knew she was really late because she didn't even make a cup of coffee.

She was getting ready to rush out the door when she stopped to give me a kiss. That's when she realized what a mess I was. She hurried to the bedroom and woke up dad. She grabbed a towel and started the sink. I knew there was no reason to fight because it was going to happen anyway, so when she came and got me I just let her do what she needed to. Dad came out and took Grace out for her walk. He wasn't out as long as normal and when he came back mum was finishing me up. She wrapped me up in a towel and handed me over to dad. She gave us both a kiss and hurried out the door.

Dad held onto me and made some coffee at the same time. When it was done he went to his desk and sat down. He told me while I warmed up and dried off I might as well learn about that fantasy football that he spent time on. He pulled up some stuff on his computer and did his research. He kept asking me which players I thought were going to have the best day tomorrow, but I didn't know. I hoped he did though because the better they did the more treats I'd be getting. When he got done with that he told me that mums birthday was going to be in just a few days again. He told me that just like last year, she would be turning twenty-nine again. He pulled up something else on his computer that had lots of pictures of flowers and asked me which ones I thought mum would like the most. We decided together and dad made the order.

When mums birthday got there dad told me we'd picked out the perfect flowers because mum absolutely loved them. I thought they looked even nicer than they did on the computer so I had to agree with him. Dad made sure to get her birthday cards from me, Leroy, Amelia and Grace again too. She always thought that was sweet and it got us extra treats and luvins every time.

It was around that time that I started getting really picky with my food again. Gramma had come for a couple of lunch dates and all I ate was a couple of bites before I turned around and faced Blankets Mountain to let her know I was done. Mum thought maybe I was getting bored with the food again. Instead of trying to find a different type of food she had a different idea. She got a couple of jars of baby food and mixed some of that in with my regular food. That smelled so different that I had to try it. When I did I thought it was delicious and I ate so much mum had to make me stop so I wouldn't get sick.

Dad figured that if I was getting bored with my food that it might be time to change up some of my toys too. He started looking around for some of my favorite toys that had been missing for a while. He dug around under the couch and started finding all kinds of things. One of the things he found was one of my favorite blue feathers that I liked to chase at night. He also got a brand new peacock feather out that one of my friends sent me. Dad said he had been saving it for a special occasion. He told mum he would surprise me with it later that night. He didn't know I already spotted it, but I would make sure I acted surprised when he gave it to me. Mum and dad sure are smart and always manage to figure out how to keep me happy. I appreciated that and loved them very much.

One night while mum was helping me do my evening Facebook post, one of my friends sent a picture of me dressed up like a pirate. He said it was national talk like a pirate day. Mum heard it was also world peace day. Mum had already finished my post but she thought the picture was so cute she decided to do another one. I decided I would celebrate both of those special days at the same time by making up my own holiday. I declared it Pirates for Peace day! Mum said since I'm so cute I can get away with making up my own holidays. Since I made it up myself I decided that Pirates for Peace Day must be celebrated with feathers and beef stick treats! I was going to have to start thinking up more holidays to celebrate.

The next weekend dad was watching movies while he planned out his fantasy football strategies for Sunday. Since they were on the television we were watching what dad said was the original Star Wars trilogy. Dad said that it's important for every little boy to watch them because they're classics. Mum said she's not so sure about all that but she didn't fuss that dad was watching them. After the first movie was over, I thought that someone needed to share some feathers with the angry guy with the breathing problem so he could be happy.

Neuro Dan - Feather Dan

October 25, 2016 ·

Hai my furiends. Iz in a good mood and playful tonight but I wasn't at all hungry today. I only ate about half of what I should for gramma at our lunch date. I ate even less for dinner. Iz chomping down treats and I'm getting lots of them too. Mum says that if I don't eat better tomorrow she's taking me in to the vet. While I like my vet and everyone there is super sweet to me I really don't like going. Do you know the first thing they always want to do? Check my temperature. Do you know HOW they check my temperature??? Not cool!!! I talked to dad and he said when he has to go to the vet they check his temperature by clicking something in his ear. So what the heck guys? We cats have ears too! I say again, not cool! Well Iz off to play FEATHERS and gobble up a bunch of treats now. Sleep with the angels tonight my friends. I luvs you all.

The next Sunday I was hanging out with dad while he watched his football games. Whoever he was rooting for must have been doing really good because I got tons of treats. He even spent extra time playing feathers with me. Later, mum got home and watched the games with dad. By the end of the day, they were both in a great mood so I guessed that both their teams won again. In fact, dad liked football so much that I decided that it must be his version of playing with feathers. I thought feathers were a better idea because football didn't last all year long and feathers did.

That night I saw the biggest bug I'd ever seen in my entire life. It must have been as big as Leroy's entire head! I couldn't tell what kind it was. It looked like a mutant mix of moth, beetle and fly! It must have come in with dad when he and Grace came back from their walk. It flew down the hall, past the cat tree and towards the bedroom. I watched it as it turned around, flew back into the living room, and then zipped into the kitchen. I got super excited, stood up and goose honked right at it.

That got mums attention really quick and she started looking around to see what got me excited. She didn't see the bug, but when dad came back into the living room she told him something had me excited and I just goose honked. Dad was walking to the kitchen to get a drink when the mutant bug flew back out. It flew right towards dads head! He saw it and ducked. Mum saw it too and let out a little scream. That made Grace bark. She jumped up to her feet and started looking around.

Leroy had been eating his dinner. He didn't see the bug when it first flew in, but he saw it when dad ducked. He chattered at it and jumped from the kitchen table. He then leapt into the air to try to catch it. He missed and almost landed on dads back before he plummeted to the floor. That was when Grace saw it and she started barking. All of the excitement was too much and I goose honked at it again.

Amelia came running into the living room from the bedroom to see what was going on. She saw the bug right away. It was flying towards the cat tree and television area in the living room. She scrambled up the cat tree and swatted towards it but it was too far away. Leroy raced into the living room right behind it. He jumped up onto dad's desk and sent the mail that was sitting there scattering across his desk and all over the living floor.

Mum yelled for dad to get that thing out of the house. Dad was looking at it trying to figure out what the heck it was. He told mum it looked like Mothra from the Godzilla stories and wanted to know how she thought he should show it the door. It landed on the wall above the television for just a minute and both Leroy and Amelia pounced at it in unison. Leroy jumped up from the desk and Amelia dropped down from the cat tree. They both landed behind the television and it started to wobble. Dad moved quickly and steadied the TV before it could fall off the stand.

The commotion had Grace barking nonstop. Mum was sitting close to me and still telling dad to get it out of the house. I agreed with mum. He better figure it out soon before Leroy and Amelia wrecked the entire living room trying to catch it. More importantly, I wanted it gone before it swooped down and flew off with my Temptations! The bug flew off the wall above the TV and headed toward mum's desk. Dad grabbed the TV again as Leroy and Amelia scrambled out from behind it.

Mums desk was the next victim of this hilarious pursuit. Dad hurried into the kitchen and came back out with the broom. The bug had landed on the ceiling right in the middle of the living room. Leroy and Amelia were sitting directly under it staring upward. Grace was barking at it. I really wanted to know what dad was going to do with the broom and boy I found out right away. He pushed Grace out of the way so he could get a good angle on it and gave the ceiling a swat.

The bug jumped for it right as the broom struck. Dad still got it and he sent it spinning through the air and right at me and mum! Mum screamed and covered her face. It tumbled right between us! I could see its wings beating and trying to regain its balance. I jumped up and took a swat at it as it tumbled past me. I was just a little bit out of range and missed but I thought that was lots of fun. Leroy and Amelia charged at the couch right at me and mum. Leroy jumped over both of us and landed on the floor behind us. Amelia ran right over mum!

Mum screamed again then said some more words at dad that I should have covered my ears for. Dad apologized and hurried around the other side of the couch. The bug landed on the kitchen table with Leroy right behind it. Leroy pounced again, but the bug took off. Leroy pounced so hard he slid across the table and knocked their food bowl off the edge. It landed right next to Graces food bowl and the water bowl. Pieces of food scattered everywhere.

Dad was pretty quick and as the bug tried to fly back into the living room he smacked it before it could get past him. He sent it flying down the hall towards the front door. It landed on the floor and this time, Amelia tried to get it. She got caught on one of dad's feet as he went back after it and got the equivalent of the pit maneuver while he was trying to get the bug. She spun out and crashed into the wall. Grace was right behind dad barking at the bug but she didn't try to push past him. He got the bug with the broom and held it down while he opened the door. He stepped back and gave the bug one quick swat like he was sweeping really hard. He caught the bug and it launched out the front door. He then quickly stepped forward and slammed the door shut.

That was fun! I thought dad should go back out and find another one just like it. That was almost as fun as playing feathers. Leroy and Amelia stayed on high alert for the rest of the night. They were constantly looking around to make sure that bug didn't have a friend still hiding in the house. I don't think it did because another one never did come out to play. Mum told dad he did good, but next time, please avoid swatting the nasty bugs at her. Dad said he hadn't meant to and sat down with us. I was super excited and frisky after all that and played extra hard with my feathers for the rest of the night.

Later that week I found out mum and dad had a wedding anniversary coming up. Mum was doing what she does every year right before their anniversary. She had their wedding album out and was showing me all of the pictures. Mum and dad sure did look different in those pictures. They were celebrating their 20th wedding anniversary that year. Mum said that was a long time ago and the reason they looked so different was because they were much younger then.

,

I always liked it when mum pulled out the photo albums and sat down to look at them with me. This time, it made me remember my own past and I wondered how JuJu was doing. I hoped she loved her life as much as I loved mine. I knew whoever got her would have a best friend for life so I was sure she was fine. Mum said that my Facebook page was like my very own photo album. Mum liked to go back through that once in a while too to look at those pictures. I liked the way she would sit and share with me anytime she did something like that.

A few days later and the day after their anniversary, mum's sister came up from Florida for a visit. Well, it wasn't really a scheduled visit, but mum always liked to see family when they were in town. This time they were coming because there was a hurricane headed towards where they lived and they didn't want to get caught in it. Mum said they lived in a place close Jacksonville, Florida and every now and then, big storms came through. She said this one was so big it was dangerous and she was glad that the family was coming home instead of riding it out. I remembered when mum showed me where all of my Facebook friends lived that I had lots that lived in Florida. I made sure to tell all of them to be safe on my Facebook post that night.

When mums sister came over to visit, she had a small dog with her. I thought he was funny looking because he didn't really have a tail. Mum said he was a Boston Terrier and that his name was Recon. He was a very friendly dog and got along pretty well with Grace. He was scared to death of the cats though. Mum told me grammas cats didn't like him one bit. They would chase him and keep him cornered on her couch when he visited there. I thought he was odd looking. I know it isn't exactly polite to look, but without a tail, it was just impossible not to notice. I didn't say anything in front of him because I didn't want to hurt his feelings but he had the biggest butt hole that I had ever seen. It was bigger than Graces and she was easily four times his size! That back end was dangerous too. He had the worst case of gas ever! I hoped this was giving mum and dad a better appreciation for me on those few occasions when I cleared the room. Mum said Recon did this all the time. I couldn't imagine having to have chronic farts. I learned to appreciate my neurological issues a bit more that day.

The next week when dad got home, he sat down with me. He told me that mum was having what people called "one of those days". She had some ugly things happen at work and she was really upset. Dad told me that because she worked with children who had been taken into state custody because of various reasons that she was exposed to a lot of very difficult things to see and hear. She was pretty good at her job and usually she wasn't terribly affected by it. Every once in a while, a case would come up that was just too ugly for her not to be upset over. As a result, she was having "one of those days".

I told dad we'd have to team up to get her mind off of work. I made him a deal. I told him I'd give her my sweet eyes and extra belly rubs time and he could give her one of my beef stick treats and feathers. I didn't think there was any way she could stay in a bad mood with beef sticks treats and feathers. Dad told me that it was a good idea but maybe we should get mum a bottle of wine and some chocolate instead. I disagreed and told him to trust me about the treats and feathers.

When mum got home we put our plan into action. The sweet eyes worked right away and rolling over for belly rubs made her smile. She talked to me and dad for quite a while. When it was finally couch time, dad brought out a bottle of wine and a box of chocolates. I couldn't believe dad didn't listen to me! Mum gave him a hug. They opened the wine and the chocolates. Once they sat back down, dad got a feather and a beef stick treat and told her those were from me. Whew! I guess it was okay to do both, but I was pretty sure the beef stick treats and feathers were the best way to make her smile. As it turned out I was right. She got a good laugh out of it and I got more belly rubs.

Over the next couple of days, mums mood improved and she got back to normal. One night she and dad were talking about what to watch on TV. They were trying to decide if they should watch a presidential debate or not. When I heard them agree that they should at least watch some it I groaned. Ugh! I didn't want to watch that nonsense. Those people were always arguing with each other, talking over each other and none of them sounded like they were very honest to begin with. I thought life was too short to act like they did.

I couldn't understand the whole politics thing. I thought the entire concept sounded silly. Only people could agree to make up rules that made life more confusing and then sit there and argue with each other about what the rules meant. I thought it was entirely ridiculous and a complete waste of time. I wished I could tell them that life is too short and precious to act like they do. I gave mum and dad a stern look to let them know I disagreed with the night's entertainment and that there better be lots of feathers and extra treats to make up for it. I thought hard about taking the remote, changing the channel to something with Jackson Galaxy and not letting them have it back until tomorrow. They must have agreed with me because after a while they decided to watch something else, which I appreciated very much.

Over the next week, two things happened. I got in a really good mood, which made me a lot more playful than normal. I wound up going on extra floor adventures. I decided to spend time playing with those toys dad set up that were dangling from the cat tree. I was having so much fun with them that Leroy and Amelia even played along with me.

The other thing that happened was I lost my appetite again. Mum was pretty confused because I was so energetic and active. I was only eating about half my food before I turned around to let them know I was done. I wouldn't eat a full meal for anyone; not even gramma. Of course that got me extra treats. It even got me some of those special liquid treats that mum saved for emergencies like what she said I was doing now. They tried several different foods but none of them really got my attention.

Mum began to wonder if my neurological condition was bothering me in some way. I wasn't moving any different but she knew that just because she couldn't see a change, that didn't mean something wasn't happening. She told dad she wanted him to come up with a way to feed me somewhere else. She wondered if I was just having trouble moving my head and she just couldn't see it. Dad said he'd figure something out.

It was a lot more difficult to figure out then he thought it was going to be. I am very picky about how my body is situated when I eat. I have to be or I tend to choke or drop all of my food all over myself. He tried stacking cushions and blankets in all kinds of different shapes and forms. He would set me down and see if I would take a bite. I wasn't eating, but I was very entertained watching him spend an entire day building different dinner tables for me. He was about to post a video of me eating to my Facebook page and ask my friends for suggestions when he finally put together a set up that worked. I made a huge mess but ate a little more than I had been. He let mum know and she said she was bringing home some more different food again.

The next morning she fed me some salmon and I did eat more of that than the others they tried and that gave her an idea. She got a can of tuna fish and mixed some of it in with my next meal. That worked really well and I ate almost all of it! Mum felt much better and told me that if I gave them any more difficulty with the eating I was going back to the vet. I had a lunch date with gramma the next day and she heated my lunch up for me. That made it smell delicious and I ate every single bite of my lunch. Gramma told mum what she did and mum thought that was a great idea.

I started eating better again right after that. I had a few friends let mum know that too much tuna could be bad for my kidneys, so the extra tuna got phased out pretty quickly. I started eating on my ledge again without any difficulty and dad put the setup he created away so it wasn't cluttering the living room. I was still in a great mood and full of energy. I went on several floor adventures. Dad kept my steps pushed up against the glass door during the day and I went back to sitting on top of those and watching the birds fly and leaves blow around during the day.

Everyone was still talking about why I had been having such a hard time with my food. I couldn't really answer the question because I didn't know myself. It was just one of those neurological things that get in my way now and then. I was just grateful that it had passed and I was back to normal again. I could tell by how worried everyone had been that mum, dad and gramma sometimes had a harder time coping with the disease than I did. I wished that they didn't have to worry so much and try so hard to help me, but I knew they loved me and never thought twice about it. They just did what needed to be done.

Neuro Dan - Feather Dan
November 8, 2016 ·

Hai my furiends. I had a good day. Gramma came over and visited tonight and she gave me yummy beef stick treats. I got another new food to try that was real good. I like that my food has so much variety now. Iz practicing my grrrrrrr face in case people don't get along tonight. Mum says there's this thing called an election and sometimes people get a bit carried away with their emotions. I says I will share my FEATHERS and Temptations (but maybe not the beef stick treats) with anyone having a bad day. But just in case that doesn't work this my "you better behave or else" face. Time to get after some FEATHERS now! Sleep with the angels tonight my friends. I luvs you all.

October ended quietly for us. Mum and dad got ready for Halloween and the trick or treaters that would be out. They had several bags of candy ready to hand out and left the porch light on to let the kids know it was okay to stop by. As it turned out we only got two families that night. Mum found out later after asking on Facebook that the town did something new that year which became very popular with the families. They held an event in a parking lot where people could park and trick or treat at all of the car's trunks. They called it Trunk or Treat. There were still some popular neighborhoods where they went to as well, but mum said that Trunk or Treat was a good idea and probably much safer. If the children weren't running around the streets, they'd be less likely to get hit by a car. Mum and dad sure did have lots of leftover candy to eat though. If they were going to do it again next year, I was going to recommend they get Temptations just in case there was so much leftover again.

We barely made it through Halloween before the weather started to change. The temperature dropped fast and the wind started to pick up. Mum said a big cold front was moving in. She sat down with me and gave me some luvins. She told me not to stress over the change in temperature and asked me what she could do to help. Rapid temperature changes, especially cold fronts, tended to cause my neurological condition to act up. I thought about it and got an idea.

She must have remembered the same thing because she jumped up and went to the hall closet. She rummaged through it for a minute and came back out with my heated cat bed and the electric blanket. She spread the electric blanket across the back of the couch and put my heated cat bed down in front of the glass door. She plugged the electric blanket in and I didn't waste any time at all. I walked over and climbed right up. It only took a few minutes before I could feel the wonderful heat starting to build up. A few minutes later I sprawled out with my belly up and purred loudly to tell her thank you.

The weather was still getting worse by the next day. The wind was blowing hard and leaves were whipping all over the yard. They looked like big jumping feathers so I decided to go on a floor adventure and perch on my heated cat bed. I could feel the cold through the glass but the heated cat bed kept me plenty warm. Every now and then a bunch of brown and red leaves would blow into the porch and rattle against the glass door. They surprised Grace at one point and she started barking at it. That startled me but I thought she was being funny after a minute. She lay down next to me and watched the leaves blow for the rest of the day.

Gramma had made a trip back to Florida with mum's sister a week ago and I sure was missing my lunch dates with her. When she finally got back, she surprised me in the middle of the day when she walked in the door. Mum already fed me my breakfast so this wasn't a lunch date. She just missed me and wanted to come by and tell me hi. She carried me over to the glass door and watched the leaves blow around while she told me how much fun she had on her trip. She even took all of her kitties with her. She said it was quite the car ride with her, gramma-great and three cats. I couldn't imagine that long of a car ride. She said it was even farther away than when I went to Auburn. I made sure she got extra wet face mushes and got her glasses extra hard so she'd know I loved her and missed her too.

That night something scary but remarkable happened. It was well after midnight and I was busy cleaning my tail on top of Blankets Mountain. Leroy and Amelia had already done one round each of those odd random patrols. Like usual, I watched them to try to figure out what they were looking out for and like usual, nothing happened.

Amelia came out of the bedroom for her next patrol later that night. She walked along the walls of the living room. She went behind the closed blinds at the sliding glass door; then behind mum's desk. She came out and circled the coffee table, then hopped up on the couch. She walked along the top by the wall and dropped down onto the floor. She made her way into the kitchen, came out, wandered through the dining room and started down the hall.

She got two steps down the hall and stopped. Her ears went flat on her head, the fur on her back stood up and her tail poofed out like a Christmas tree. She arched her back and gave out a very long drawn out scary sounding hiss. She poofed herself up even taller and gave a savage growl.

I jumped up and strained my neck to try to see over Amelia. She wasn't playing around or just trying to be mean; she was genuinely in battle mode. I finally saw something moving on the floor a few feet in front of her down the hall near the front door. It was dark but I had great night vision and once I focused on it I got a good look. It was a snake!

Holy cat! How the heck did a snake get in the house?? It slithered towards her a bit. It was moving cautiously. The snakes head was up and its tongue kept darting in and out testing the air around it. It would slither a few inches forward and stop. Amelia didn't back up. She held her ground and let loose a loud, guttural howling growl. She hissed so hard that spit flew from her mouth towards the snake.

I watched in amazement. I'd never seen a real snake in person before. I wondered if it was one of the poisonous ones and how you could tell the difference. I didn't know how it got in and I was really worried about what it was going to do. I wasn't about to let Amelia fight it off on her own. We needed dad or Grace to help us out. I was trying to figure out if I should go help Amelia or if I should try to go to the bedroom and wake up Grace. If I could get Grace up she would bark and get dad up.

I started to back myself down and off of Blankets Mountain. I decided I would figure it out when I got to the hall. If the snake was trying to get Amelia I'd go help her fight it off. If she still had it held at bay, then I'd go get Grace. I barely had time to get turned around to back down when I heard the bedroom door bang against the wall.

I looked and Leroy was charging down the hall towards Amelia. He glanced at me and yelled for me to stay up on Blankets Mountain. With just a few leaps, Leroy's long strides got him side by side with Amelia. He looked at the snake and hissed. Leroy didn't hiss very often and when he did he reminded me of a tiger. His hiss always had a bit of a growl mixed in with it that was meant to let it be known he was in charge.

The snakes tongue flickered in and out again and it slithered forward a few more inches. Leroy responded by stepping forward. He put himself between Amelia and the snake. He gave one more growling hiss. It was a loud drawn out hiss that lasted longer than any hiss I'd ever heard. The snake responded by moving forward another few inches before it stopped. It was only about two feet in front of Leroy. Leroy raised his right paw and I could see his claws were already out. It had been a little while since mum had trimmed our nails so I knew his claws would be extremely sharp.

Its tongue flicked in and out and the snake slithered forward one more time. Leroy responded with another hiss. He crouched low close to the ground so he could either pounce or spring back. Cautiously he began to move forward. The snake must have finally realized the danger it was in because it struck forward at Leroy.

The strike was incredibly fast but didn't come close to striking Leroy. Leroy never even flinched. The snake quickly coiled up into a defensive posture and hissed back at Leroy. Leroy was in predator mode. Staying crouched low to the ground he stalked the snake. His ears were flat, his whiskers forward. He stalked carefully. He moved one foot forward and stopped. He moved another foot forward and stopped. He did that several times. Each of his moves were calculated, each step was deliberate. His body was tense, his muscles ready to respond at any moment.

He finally got close enough to the snake that it struck out at him again. I've never seen Leroy move so fast in my life. His right paw lashed out and swatted the snake's head to the side. The strike was hard enough that it unbalanced the snake for just a second. Leroy pounced immediately. It was a short leap, only about one foot forward. His entire body landed on the snake and his right paw caught the snake in the head again. With one final strike, Leroy put a single claw through the center of the snake's skull.

The snake tossed and turned but Leroy was on top of it and he held it down. He held his claw in place for a minute until the snake went still. He dragged it down the hall and left it in the middle of the area between the dining room and the kitchen. Mum and dad wouldn't be able to miss it when they got up in the morning. Then he retracted his claw. He sat down in front of the snake and began to groom. Amelia stayed behind Leroy until he was finished, then left to finish her patrol.

Neither Leroy nor Amelia went back to bed that night. They stayed up and alert. They did a lot more patrols than normal, but never found another snake. I asked Leroy if that was the reason they did their patrols every night. He said it was and that there had been two other snakes that had gotten in throughout the years. He said the last one got in just a couple of weeks before I first arrived. He could never figure out where they were getting in from but he and Amelia had made a pact that they would keep the house safe. That was why they did the patrols.

I told him I would start doing patrols with them. Now that I knew what to look for I would help out too. Leroy told me that if I saw a snake I was to leave it alone and get him. I told him I could hold my own, but he told me that they might be poisonous and mum and dad would be devastated if anything happened to me. I told Leroy they would be just as upset if something happened to him so I didn't think it was a reasonable request.

We argued back and forth for a while and he finally made me promise to keep a look out from Blankets Mountain. He told me that the snakes, for whatever reason, always wound up coming down the hall towards the living room. He said my vantage point from Blankets Mountain would be the perfect lookout spot. His main goal was to make sure neither mum nor dad got surprised and bit by a snake. He said he'd killed the previous two and he was an expert snake fighter.

He reminded me that the goal was to keep mum and dad safe and that we each had to do the part we would be best at. He was best at fighting but I would be best at seeing them if they ever showed up again. I thought about that and I had to agree. We each had to contribute in the best way we could. That's what made teams great. I was impressed that the big guy could articulate and debate so well with me. He was normally not much for words but he could be convincing when his mind was set.

Dad was the first one up in the morning. He came out of the bedroom with Grace right on his heels. He was about to grab her leash off the kitchen table when he spotted the snake on the ground. He stopped dead in his tracks and stared at it for a second. Grace saw it too and walked quickly walked up to give it a sniff. Dad shewed Grace away and poked at the snake with his shoe. Once he realized it was dead he got some paper towels. He wrapped it up and took it outside. It took him a minute before he came back inside. Once he got back in, Grace was whining and hopping up and down at him. She really had to do her business. Dad grabbed the leash and out the door they went.

Mum got up while dad was still out with Grace. She went into the kitchen and made them both a cup of coffee. She set dads on his desk and went to her desk with hers. Dad came back in and told mum about finding the snake on the floor. Mum wasn't very happy to hear about that. She asked if it was a poisonous snake. Dad told her it wasn't; he was pretty sure that it was just a black snake. It had been young and only about a foot and a half long.

Mum said that was long enough and she asked if dad thought Leroy got it again. Dad told her yes and that it only had one mark on it; a hole right through the center of its head and out the bottom of the jaw. They talked about how it had been a long time since one had gotten in again. Mum came over and sat with me and gave me luvins. She asked if I had seen the snake and I excitedly stood up and turned circles, then sat back down and looked at where Leroy had dragged it.

Mum got up and called for Leroy. It didn't take long for him to come running. She got into her desk and got out the Temptations.

As soon as Amelia heard the drawer open she came running too. She gave us all treats and dad gave Grace a new bone. I thought it was great that we were getting treats before we even got our breakfast. Leroy was looking very proud of himself. He rubbed up against mums legs several times. Mum gave him head scratches. He hopped up on the coffee table and sprawled out.

Leroy and Amelia stepped up their patrols for the next several days. They did twice as many as normal. I stayed vigilant too. I took Leroy's advice and kept an eye out from Blankets Mountain. I really did have a great vantage point from there. I could see the entire living room, most of the dining room, all the way down the hall to the closet in mum and dads bedroom and all the way down the other end of the hall to the front door.

The snake added a new element to my life. It never occurred to me that something like that could get inside. I asked Leroy how he could tell if they were poisonous but he said he didn't know. He treated them all like they were a threat to mum and dad. He said he didn't like killing, but he did what needed to be done. He tried hissing and growling first to let it know it needed to leave. If it didn't leave immediately he wasn't taking any chances.

He told me that Mum and Dad protected them and took care of them in their way. Grace was a great guard dog and protected the family in her own way. He said that being cats we are great hunters and we have a duty to protect the family in our own way. Guarding against snakes was a very important duty. He didn't tell me what those patrols were all about when I first got here because he wanted me to be able to feel safe in a new home. He knew I would be scared and with my neurological condition he didn't see any reason to stress me out over it.

Now that I knew he reminded me that I was now part of the patrol. My job was lookout and I shared in the responsibility to keep mum and dad safe. It felt good to be part of the patrol and to know I was helping to keep mum and dad safe. I would take my responsibility very seriously. I loved mum and dad greatly and if I could, I would do anything to keep them safe.

Neuro Dan - Feather Dan
· December 15, 2016 ·

Soooo. Yes. She did this to me. Yes I posed but only because she said she would take it off after she got a pic. Mum checked the mail today. Iz got 15 cards!! Iz got pics of kitties like Mabel and Cheeto. Iz got loves and well wishes. And I got 2 huge packages of presents. Those presents had to be wrapped by a professional. It took mum 30 minutes to get them opened. Dad and I laughed at her. This outfit was in there too. Iz love you all so much. I hope you know that. Sleep with the angels my furiends. You mean so very much to me. 🎅❤❤

Of all of the traditions and holidays that people celebrate Thanksgiving is my most favorite. I know most people are just too busy to be able to stop every day and think about the things that they are thankful for. I believe that because they have the insight to set aside even one day a year to slow down and remember all of our blessings show that people really do have tremendous insight into what is important in life.

Then there are the feathers. Thanksgiving means turkey and turkeys have feathers. I asked mum how many feathers a turkey has. She didn't know but she looked it up and told me that they can have 6000 feathers! Oh my Cat that's a lot of chomping! I thought about that for a minute and wondered if I could figure out how to make a turkey trap. I'd also have to figure out where all of those turkeys lived. I had never seen a live turkey before. I'd have to ask outside cat DJ if he had seen them around. I decided that I could probably use a blanket to throw over the turkey. If I could just slow it down and make it flap its wings extra hard I bet a feather or two would fall off. I asked dad to set up a trap for me in the back yard just in case.

On Thanksgiving mum and dad went over to grammas to celebrate with the family. Just like last year it took them several trips to get all of the food they cooked carried up to the car. That food sure did smell good all day while they were cooking. They came home several hours later. Once they brought several trips worth of leftovers back inside mum gave me a surprise.

I guess dad must have set out my blanket trap and it actually worked because mum had a real turkey feather! I spent the rest of the day chomping on that feather and giving mum the eyes to try to get extra bites of the leftovers. Mum told me no to leftovers. She said she remembered what happened last year and she didn't want to go through that mess again. Once I thought about it I had to agree with her because last year I got too much and it resulted in a sink bath. I didn't want any more sink baths than were absolutely necessary. I decided it was smarter to settle for some turkey flavored treats instead.

Another cold front started to move in. It took two days for it to finally settle in and right before it did we got hit with some really bad storms. While I enjoyed watching the leaves blowing around while the front came in I wasn't as much of a fan of the thunder boomers that came with it. Mum was surprised and relieved that the cold front didn't bother my neuro condition like it normally did. She told me she was impressed by how good I did the night the thunderstorm hit. I didn't like it but I didn't cry at her or try to hide. I even went belly up on Blankets Mountain to enjoy my heated blanket.

I did really well with the change in weather and the storms but poor dad didn't fare as well. The cold front came in and two days later he was sick. Mum said he got sick just in time for the weekend. Unfortunately for dad, mum had to work that weekend. That meant it was going to be up to me to take care of dad. I decided that I was going to go all out. I was pretty sure that my Temptations would work like vitamins so every time he gave me some I was going to tell him to have some too. I even planned on sharing Blankets Mountain and my heated blanket with him.

Mum listened to my plan and told me that I probably didn't have to go to such extreme lengths. She assured me that some snuggle time on the couch with him watching movies was probably going to be more than enough. I wasn't going to take any chances. That night I even asked my Facebook friends if they had any suggestions on what to do to help sick dads feel better. I got lots of good ideas! I was sure, if nothing else, I would be able to use them to help dad pass the time.

I did my best that weekend to try to help dad feel better. He didn't seem to want any of my Temptations and he gave me a funny look when I asked him if he wanted to sit on Blankets Mountain. He did like it when I gave him snuggle time and kisses. My friends recommended I try that and they were right he relaxed and even took a nap.

Even though he was sick he still did a great job of keeping up with my meals. Earlier in the week he bought a variety pack of food and was trying some of that. I really liked that. Once I realized how good it was I decided that I wanted extra and wanted to eat early. I tried to get dads attention to let him know I was ready. I jumped up every time he walked by hoping he'd get the hint that I wanted to eat early but he didn't seem to get it.

I remembered that mum said sometimes with dads you have to be very blunt about what you want. When he sat down with his lunch I gave him one big loud meow. That got his attention and as soon as he finished his sandwich I got a big plate of my wet food. I did that big loud meow at supper too and surprised mum that time. It worked and I got an extra big dinner. Mum told dad that his plan to fatten me up might just work. I thought it was working pretty well because I was getting super big plates of the yummy food. I was even getting a few extra treats at night.

I was getting extra full and that meant a few more after dinner naps. It was really hard to stay awake with a full belly and stretching out on the heated blanket. It didn't stop me from being fully awake and ready for my nightly feathers time though. I was extra frisky one night and mum took a video of me jumping up after a feather. I told her I was doing expert tiger pounces but she told me I looked like I was doing frog hops again. I assured her they were most certainly not frog hops. She put the video on my Facebook page that night and tried to tell everyone I was doing frog hops but I corrected them and let them know it was a tiger pounce. They got a good laugh out of it which made me happy. It always felt really good to make my friends smile.

It was starting to get closer to Christmas time. It was just a couple of weeks away. The poor mailman was probably getting frustrated with me again. I started getting a lot of cards in the mail. I was getting more than I ever had before. Mum and dad had to be sure that one of them checked the mail every day to keep up or the mailman wouldn't have room to put anything else. She sat down with me every night and opened them up. She'd show me each one and read them out loud so I could hear the stories. I was surprised how many handwritten notes I was getting. My friends sure did know how to make me feel special and loved. Mum said I had a lot more friends now than I did the year before and they must really love me.

I was having a great stretch of really good days. My neuro issues weren't bothering me and I was in a great mood. I was eating great and put on a little bit of weight which made mum extra happy. The good days didn't stop but I wound up having to get a sink bath. The new food was catching up to my digestive system and I wound up with diarrhea. I just can't move quick enough to get out of it when that happens and my back legs wind up getting dirty.

Mum got a different baby shampoo to use on me and while I had to admit I smelled really nice afterwards it sure did take a long time to clean myself up and get my fur perfect again. I also got extra treats on days where I had to get a bath. I made sure I gave her the eyes and it worked great. Mum gave in and I got two beef stick treats that night.

I managed to avoid getting messy the next day but not so much the day after. Yup, I got stuck getting two sink baths that week. Mum was trying to figure out what to do. She told me I was going to have to go visit the vet if my bathrooms didn't get better pretty soon. She was already adding something she called FortiFlora to my food. That helped great with the old food but not so much with the new stuff that I was enjoying so much. She tried putting some pumpkin in my food but yuck! Who wants pumpkin with their salmon? I'm pretty sure the answer to that is no one and neither did I. She told dad she was debating putting me back on my old food but she knew I wouldn't eat as well if she did. She finally asked my Facebook friends if any of them had any ideas. They gave her lots of suggestions and she and I both were hoping some of them would help.

I'm not sure how I didn't hear mum and dad talking about it but I got a huge surprise. It was the middle of the day, gramma had already come over to feed me lunch and I heard the front door open up. I knew mum and dad wouldn't be home yet so I stood up and stretched while I waited to see who was coming in. Grace ran over as soon as she heard the key in the door and of course she was barking. As soon as the door opened she started jumping up and down with her tail wagging.

Both of my grammas came through the door! Gramma came in first and got Grace to back up. That gave my Grammy a chance to get her luggage inside before she got jumped on. She barely got the door shut before Grace was jumping up at her trying to give her big sloppy tongue kisses. Grammy told her hi and pet her for a minute then gramma got the treat bag out and called for Grace. She ran right over and got a brand new chew bone. She tossed it in the air the pounced on it. She turned so she could see everyone and sat down to chew her bone.

Both grammas came over to say hi to me. I was so happy I was purring loud and I made sure to give both of them big wet faced mushes. Leroy was curious about the talking and came out of the bedroom. He was still half asleep and blinking sleep out of his eyes. Amelia trotted up and jumped up on the couch to say hi. Gramma went to the mum's desk and got a bag of treats out of the drawer. We all got extra treats and luvins. Grammas talked for a few minutes and then gramma told Grammy she was going to go home and let her get settled in.

When mum got home she asked Grammy if she saw the video she posted of my frog hops. I couldn't believe mum was still calling them frog hops! I was going to explain this to Grammy during feathers time and show her that they look more like savage tiger pounces. She got a good laugh when I did and she told me they were very good tiger pounces. I knew I didn't look like a goofy frog and I was glad Grammy set the record straight.

The next day I worked it for all it was worth. Grammy was extra susceptible to me giving her the sweet eyes. I got so many treats that mum was worried I wasn't going to eat for dinner but she was wrong. I was determined to show off for Grammy. I did a great job at dinner and ate really well. Grammy was definitely impressed by how much I was eating. We even got to watch one of my favorite movies. Grammy hadn't seen Pete's Dragon yet and she said she liked it as much as I did.

By Sunday mum said I had been one spoiled boy that weekend. I told her I didn't mind being spoiled and actually I liked it. I told her she should be taking notes from Grammy on how many treats I should be getting every day. I got a new kind of treat in the mail the same day Grammy showed up. Mum said it was called a Royal Canin treat. I was flattered that I was getting treats that were made for royalty. They sure were good and Grammy had given me lots. Grammy was going to be leaving on Tuesday so I only had a couple days left to show off for her. I made sure to do my tiger pounces so she'd keep telling mum they weren't frog hops.

The next day mum, dad and Grammy were gone most of the day. I showed off and ate a really big lunch but I was hungry by the time they came home. When they did come home they were over an hour late in getting me my dinner. Since Grammy had to go home tomorrow they took dad out to Joes Crab Shack for an early birthday dinner. They smelled delicious when they got back. They smelled like yummy crab which is one of my favorite foods. I had to fuss at mum for not bringing me back my own plate. Mum told me the crab food I get is different and actual crab is not on my current diet. Plus she reminded me crabs didn't have feathers so they didn't have anything for me that trip.

It sure had been a fun weekend having Grammy around. I always miss her until she gets to visit again. Mum said not everyone has a gramma that lives as close as I do who can visit as often as she does. She said a lot of people have to wait a long time in between gramma visits. Having two grammas sure is fun. I may only get to see Grammy a couple of times a year but it gives me something to look forward to.

Just a few days went by and before I knew it, it was Christmas Eve. I was so excited! I planned on staying awake so I could try to get chin scritches from Santa Paws. Mum reminded me that I'm not supposed to do that because it might ruin Christmas for all of the children. It took a minute but I remembered what she told me last year and I sure didn't want to ruin Christmas for anyone.

I had another idea though. I would leave Santa alone but I wondered if this year I could get a peek at Rudolph. I really wanted to see his bright red nose. I'd have to take it easy with the feathers chomping time if I was going to stay awake. I thought about it for a minute and had to admit that there was no way I could take it easy with the feathers. Then mum reminded me of how many presents I had to open tomorrow. She told me I was going to need my energy to get them all opened and if I didn't get enough sleep I'd be too tired to play with all the new toys. I decided to go to bed like I was supposed to so I'd be prepared for tomorrow.

Christmas morning was wonderful! I had so many packages to open that it took mum an entire hour to help me get through all of them. I had new toys of every kind imaginable! I had so many new treats and there were even some I'd never seen before. Mum and dad left to spend some of the day with family at mum's sisters. Before they left dad spread toys and feathers all over Blankets Mountain, the couch, the coffee table and the floor. Leroy and Amelia had as much fun as I did. I sure did hope all of my Facebook friends had as good of a day as I did. I hoped mum would let me know if they didn't so I could share a toy with them.

It took days to test out all of my new toys. I had to make Leroy bring back a nip toy that he ran off with. He didn't want to but it was the only one I had so I had mum go get it for me. I'd be happy to share but I thought it was only fair if he would leave it on Blankets Mountain when he was done. It was a good thing that I had so many new treats. I needed them for extra energy to keep up with all of the playing I was doing. Dad got a few days off and he spent lots of time playing with me so I could figure out which ones were my favorites.

Dad had to work on his birthday. Mum told me she hadn't said anything to him about it and he probably thought everyone forgot. His birthday was so close to Christmas that most people wished him a happy birthday when they saw him then. His birthdays were usually quiet and spent with mum, gramma and gramma great. Well of course all of us had to make sure he had fun too but we weren't lucky enough to be able to go out to eat with him.

This time mum said he was going to be surprised. There was still a lot of family in town from Christmas. Mums sister had a birthday in the middle of January. Since they were still there they decided everyone would celebrate at the same time. Mum made reservations at a steak house and when dad got home she gave him a hug and hurried him out the door. They came home and everyone came in with them. Mum, gramma, gramma great, mums sister and her husband as well as their two boys. Whew the house got full fast.

Grace was extra excited about all of the company and mums nephews had fun playing with her. Amelia didn't care for all of the extra activity and she went to the bedroom to hide out. Leroy came in and sat down by the glass door so he could watch. I stayed on top of Blankets Mountain and enjoyed the company. I hadn't seen gramma great in quite a while and she sat down next to me and we gave each other lots of luvins.

Mum got a cake out of the refrigerator and started cutting slices. The nephews forgot about Grace once the cake was cut. Gramma double checked that I hadn't left any surprises on the couch while mum was getting the cake ready so everyone could sit down. Gramma great had a very small piece of cake and she let me lick the frosting so I could taste it. It took everyone a few minutes to eat and talk and when they left mum and dad came and sat down on the couch. It was a little later than normal but dad still made sure we got to play with feathers and I even got extra treats.

It had been an exciting week. Christmas, dad's birthday, the celebration at our place was all a lot more activity then I was used to. The rest of the week went by very quickly. I knew it was almost New Year's Eve again because the neighbors behind us started to shoot off the occasional firework.

Mum surprised me and told me this year we were all going to try to stay awake and watch the ball drop. I wasn't sure what she was talking about. Last year mum and dad both had to get up early so they went to bed at their normal time. The later it got the more frequently the neighbor set off fireworks. Grace would get nervous and start pacing and barking. Leroy and Amelia stayed in the bedroom unless mum shook a treat bag. When she did that they would come out long enough to get some luvins and treats then go hide again.

I stayed on Blankets Mountain for a while but I wasn't going to let those fireworks stop me from having my feathers time. Feathers time lasted a lot longer than it usually did. Mum and dad stayed up and dad played feathers with me until I was so tired I just lay down with my belly in the air.

I finally figured out what mum meant by watching the ball drop. She also said there was something called a peach drop that happened in Atlanta. She switched back and forth between channels to see what was happening in the different cities. It was neat to see so many people out celebrating at the same time. I didn't get to see that part last year and once again I was taken aback by how much people really are more the same than different.

In the end mum and dad watched the peach drop. They gave each other a big hug and kiss and then I got hugs and kisses too. Dad got up and started turning out the lights. The neighbor was setting off a lot of fireworks now. He had as many as he did for the fourth of July and it was rattling our windows again. I'd done okay dealing with the periodic fireworks until that point but I didn't want to be alone in the dark with all of those explosions shaking the house.

I scampered up to the top of Blankets Mountain before mum could finish getting ready to go to bed. I stood up tall and gave her my loudest meow. She looked at me and came over to make sure I was okay. She knew I was going to be scared so she told dad I was coming to bed with them again. She carried me over to my spot and I did my business. Then she picked me up and carried me to the bedroom. The fireworks were still lighting up the sky and making a lot of noise but just like last year I was snuggled up between mum and dad.

I couldn't have felt safer. The fireworks would still make me flinch now and then but I wasn't trembling. Grace was letting out little barks from under the bed in protest and I could tell mum and dad weren't going to be able to sleep until they stopped either. When they finally stopped mum scratched my head for a bit then fell asleep.

Just like last year I couldn't help but to reflect on my life and what had happened that year. I could understand why people celebrated the end of a year and the beginning of another. So much happened in life that it was important to stop for a bit and just slow down. I spent quite a bit of time being grateful for my life all year. I did appreciate that there was a day set aside just for that but life was something that I was incredibly grateful for.

I realized that I had quite a bit of time to sit and think; more so even than normal cats. I also realized that I came from some pretty scary beginnings and was dealt a considerably tough hand in life. That I managed to win the lottery and find the best forever family ever gave me more to be grateful for than most. There is a kind of inner peace that comes with accepting what is and being grateful for what you have.

I was even grateful for my progressive motor neuron disease. I know that sounds strange but, like I said, I have a lot of time to spend on self-reflection. I knew the disease was likely going to result in a short life. At first it was difficult for me to think about but I knew that being angry or living in denial wasn't going to help me feel or get better. I decided that I would accept it for what it is. I mean I really didn't have any other choice did I?

Once I accepted it I found myself less afraid and more at peace. Without the fear clouding my thoughts I was able to think about other things. I thought about the things that I had because of the disease. I also started to think about the things that I wouldn't have if I didn't have the disease. I found that, in fact, pretty much everything that I loved about my life I had because of my disease.

If I hadn't been special needs KT wouldn't have thought to try to send me to mum. Mum and dad weren't looking to add another pet into to the family at the time. It was my special beginnings that got mums attention to begin with. That got her to keep track of me online. It was because my condition began to decline that KT pushed hard and kind of forced mum to take me. It was because of my special needs that mum and dad spent so much time working to get me figured out. I knew not many other humans had that kind of time to spend trying to help their pets. That extra effort helped all of us to quickly develop a deep bond with each other.

Then there are all of my Facebook friends who I really think of as my extended family. Mum never thought about making a Facebook page for Leroy, Amelia or Grace. There was nothing unique about them or their story that she thought would be something others would want to learn about. If I hadn't had my disease I would have never had anyone to tell all of my stories and adventures to. Plus, look at all of the amazing feathers and treats my

Facebook family sends me! I know not many other kitties out there get showered with that kind of love.

In the end I realized my life would be a kind of trade off. I might not live fifteen years but the years I did live were going to be remarkable. How many other cats could take on a mission to bring light to the darkness to help others who are struggling or down? Not too many, that's how many; but I could and I did. Eventually my time would come and I would have to cross the Rainbow Bridge. Until that time I would continue to spread my message of love and peace. I was small and maybe it didn't seem like I could do much I could do but I could do that. If there was anything that the world needed more of it was love and peace. If through my stories I could help do that then I would. I was honored to champion that cause.

Epilogue

Hai my furiends! I hope you enjoyed listening to the stories of the second year of my life. I had a wonderful time telling them to you. Thank you so much for taking the time to listen to me. I had such a wonderful time that year. All things considered, my neurological condition didn't bother me too much and I didn't have to go to the vet hardly at all. I was able to celebrate that JuJu found her forever home and that made me about as happy as anything could have. I had a new role in the house and was now an official part of the odd nightly patrols. Of course I was going to be a part of something that would help keep mum and dad safe!

I still have hundreds of stories left to tell. I'll take some time to gather my thoughts and try to pick out the best memories to share. Until then sleep with the angels my friends. They will protect you while you sleep. I luvs you all!

46061307R00103

Printed in Poland
by Amazon Fulfillment
Poland Sp. z o.o., Wrocław